Hannibal, Hummers & Hot Air Balloons

High performance strategies for tough times

By
William C. Jeffries

The author of *True To Type* and
*Taming the Scorpion: Preparing American Business
for the Third Millennium*

Published by:
Executive Strategies International
9620 Irishman's Run Lane
Zionsville, Indiana 46077
www.execustrat.com

Distributed by:
Executive Strategies International, Inc.

Front cover photo credits: Elephant by Jack Hollingsworth, Hummer by Bettmann/Corbis, Hot Air Balloons by Larry Brownstein

Printed in the USA

Dedication
For my son Paul: You are my sunshine!

FOREWORD

Several colleagues and friends have helped me gel my thoughts regarding High Performance. Without them, I would not have thought through as thoroughly the implications of the ideas I discuss in this book. Jeff Trenton has been a friend and colleague for over sixteen years. He is the one person I can go to for a challenging debate on metaphysics, political science, nuclear throw weight, the Northern Ireland problem, theology, sumo wrestling, Russian finances, Navy SEAL operations, tennis serves, the latest stock market outlook, or biological warfare. If I write a manuscript and believe it is off track for some reason but can't quite pinpoint why, Jeff will read it and go to the heart of the problem. A mutual friend describes him as "deceptively brilliant." She is very perceptive. It is hard to believe that one person knows so much about so many things.

Leah Dempsey was part of the Jeffries—Trenton—Dempsey waffle club fifteen years ago when we were all on the faculty of The Armed Forces Staff College, National Defense University, in Norfolk, Virginia. Over cholesterol-injected waffles and bad coffee we debated and argued politics, military intervention, ethics, sexual harassment, military special operations, Australian dating rituals, Shakespearian tragedy, and personal development for six years. Leah has this great knack for understanding the human side of inhuman events and calling me to task when I neglect them. Her continual focus on creating Team Mastery has encouraged me to continue this project for several years. When she enters a room, people are enkindled by her verve and spontaneity. Leah has an uncanny intuitive understanding of knowing who is present to help and who may be hanging around just to hinder. She is what a colleague calls, in one of his books, a "nutritious" friend—she is always there without any need to change you.

Our students who challenged us daily at that university

came from all five United States Military Services, and most federal agencies, including the Departments of State, Defense, Interior, Commerce, Justice, Health and Human Services, and Agriculture as well as those in related agencies such as the Central Intelligence Agency, Defense Mapping Agency, National Security Agency, Federal Emergency Management Agency, the National Reconnaissance Organization, and several others. Allied students were in attendance from diverse countries including Germany, England, Australia, Spain, Turkey, Mexico, Italy, the Scandinavian countries, and most of Latin America. We even had a Saudi Prince. The license plate on his Mercedes read, "# Five," indicating his in line order to the Saudi throne. Some of our ideas about leadership in culturally diverse backgrounds took root in that diverse community of learners.

Judith Noel did not see this manuscript until it was in print, but now that she has, I am sure she will recognize how much she has contributed over the years to my understanding of organizational change. She was a practicing business consultant when I was still packing a rucksack in the jungle and reading *Gravity's Rainbow* in graduate school at Duke University. Even more than the consulting insights she has provided me over the years, her counsel over the years has steeled me during times of personal trauma. We have burned up cross country and intercontinental telephone lines for hours at a time discussing life changing events in many countries. She understands, innately, what self-development and personal transitions are all about.

Celeste Zingarelli was the first person to challenge me to think more systematically about High Performance. Without her I probably would not have pursued the ideas in this book. Coming, herself, from the business world in the banking industry, Celeste has the natural insight and lingo to go with the personal magnetism that makes her such a great communicator. Her links to several graduate business schools have broadened my understanding of executive education and their contribution in helping business leaders develop a "business sense."

There are numerous other colleagues who deserve far more than passing mention. None of our ideas arrive in full blossom like Athena from the brow of Zeus. I am indebted to many people—all friends, I am delighted to say, as well as business associates. Tom Hoffman was a mentor for years in helping me to understand human dynamics. He introduced me to Marvin Weisbord and whole systems work redesign twenty years ago. Jerry Rankin's hard charging approach to life always challenges me to do everything better. Our association began years ago in Tidewater, Virginia, where every Saturday we would run an eight-mile or ten-K race and finish it off with a killer pizza and three-story brownie sundaes as we solved the problems of the world. Everything Jerry does, he engages at 110%. As one of the United States' most renowned experts in nuclear, chemical, and biological survivability, Jerry has been in great demand since the events of September 2001.

Dr. Marcy Lawton brings unimpeachable scientific credibility to everything she does. Marcy collaborated with me in some of my forays into cross-cultural work with the Myers-Briggs Type Indicator® and forced me always to look at the scientific credibility of my claims. When it comes to reengineering the workplace, the one person I can always trust to deliver financial and human results is Walt Smith. He can walk in to a manufacturing area or warehouse operation, spend a few days of diagnosis, and hand the client a check for several millions in savings. Dr. Ira Rosenberg is our virtual reality guru. His business understanding, background in R&D, and interest in web-based solutions to human discourse have revolutionized many businesses and forced me kicking and screaming into the 21st century. His insights into the power of C (collaborative)-Commerce have helped to transform our organization into a practicing virtual corporation. I learn from all of my colleagues, every time we team up with a client.

Deirdre Dempsey's keen editorial eye saved me many embarrassing slips of grammar and punctuation. She reminded me of all those rules I used to know when I was an English professor and seem to have forgotten over the years. If you should notice any remaining glitches in my text, they are fully my responsibility and most certainly slipped in after the text escaped Deirdre' s blue pencil. Kevin Yaney turned the manuscript into a book and provided savvy counsel on matters of design and aesthetics.

Most of all, I need to thank Cheryl Crawford who, in addition to being intellectually brilliant, has the finest business sense of any corporate leader I have ever known. Her understanding of the real business world challenges me every day. In every thing I talk about, she has "been there and done that." She will walk into my office and plant a seed and walk out. Later that seed will sprout into a profound business idea. She has incredible business savvy and an unimpeachable sense of integrity for which she has paid the price from time to time when working for those without the same high standards. She should be running a major corporation. The fact that she married me, and helps to raise our children, is my good luck and the corporate world's misfortune.

PREFACE

High Performance or Hype

Traditional businesses are in trouble today! Expectations are up, and profits are down. We thought the era of downsizing was the 1990's, and we all breathed a collective sigh of relief when the decade ended. The year 2000 would surely bring us good things: more job security, better wages, a shorter workweek, and higher performance if, but only if, we could spend the billions of dollars necessary to turn back the apocalyptic computer clock. The new millennium arrived devoid of all the predicted bugs, and some companies are still paying for the work done to avoid the over-hyped problems anticipated at midnight, December 31st, 2000 and again in 2001 when we learned that we had held our breath for the wrong New Year's Eve.

We spent billions of dollars to correct a potential programming problem that would occur when the second hand swept past the twelve. Millions of people stayed awake that night glued to the TV watching New Years Eve celebrations take place in several time zones around the world awaiting news of systems collapses and impending disaster. The time came and went, and there was barely a perceptible computer glitch worldwide, even in parts of Asia and Africa where no money was spent to fix a problem that may have been non-existent. Was it real or mere hype?

Meanwhile, stocks soared to new highs. P/E ratios were out of sync with reality, and first timers threw money at the stock market with unbridled enthusiasm. The economic boom continued, and IRA's grew fatter. Then, during the first year of the new millennium, not only did technology, the great motor of the economy, go into stock market freefall, but the demand for employees also fell off a cliff. What had gone wrong during the "boom" of the 1990's?

This book is the testimony of one eyewitness who saw the problems of international businesses unfolding from the boardroom to the manufacturing floor. At Union Switch and Signal, PNC, Mitsubishi Motors, GAF/ISP, Lucent Technologies, Sun Microsystems, Hoechst, Microsoft, Boeing, Harris Chemical, United Airlines, Millipore, Firestone, Petrobras, Digital, DuPont, Ford Motor Company, Great Lakes Chemical Corporation, Merck, and Kodak we saw the prevailing doctrines of economic productivity run up against the rocks. The tech wreck of the dotcoms merely prepared us for even tougher times in industrialized companies. When the Petrobras P36 oil platform sunk off the coast of Brazil in March of 2001, the oil slick left presaged the shape of things to come for many businesses which had substituted Vision and Values with enhanced profitability margins and personal greed.

Too many companies buy the popular solution: let's do what everyone else is doing. For a while the *program de jour* was the Quality Movement. Deming, Crosby, and Juran would surely cure manufacturing of all its ills. Its outgrowth in many businesses became Total Quality Management; the military and other government agencies cloned it as Total Quality Leadership. Quality Circles grew into self-managed work teams, or just plain teams, and most managers felt guilty if they were not building teams for every conceivable task.

Some cutting edge companies moved beyond teams and began talking about formal and informal mentoring programs. Meanwhile, other businesses were tiring of all of that "soft stuff" and started looking at the white space inside the wiring diagrams as the best place to wring out higher performance. Along came a bevy of consultants who preached Core Competences as the new way to improve performance. Work Redesign moved from the B-schools into the organization, Mormon theology migrated from the temple to Covey's Seven Habits, Human Resources VP's blessed Michael Hammer as the newest organizational guru, and everybody began reengineering everything. As that fad began to fade, just in the nick of time, SAP arrived on the scene to ensure that businesses would still be writing checks for millions of dollars to the big eight, then the big six, now the big five consulting companies.

Meanwhile nothing really changed. Businesses got smaller and sometimes more efficient. Analysts became more powerful, and employees felt more disenfranchised. Customers continued to demand more and more for less and less, and technology offered its Internet and intranet solutions.

The entire time, what were missing were value-centered, visionary leaders capable of anticipating and responding to the myriad of changes going on around them.

High Performance Businesses need a set of clearly articulated, agreed upon core values, a clearly stated vision of what succeeding looks like, clearly specified short and long-term goals that must be met to attain the vision, a means of measuring their progress towards the goals, and leaders capable of motivating others to execute a strategy. Very little has changed, in that regard, since Hannibal crossed the Alps. We have just traded in elephants for Hummers, hot air balloons for Boeing 777's, and blacksmith shops for corporations. While the language may have changed, companies still need to know where they are going and how to get there. That is what this book is all about. The problems occur across the broad spectrum of the organization; likewise, so do the solutions.

I will begin by looking at organizational change. Nobody likes it, but we have all experienced it. Next, I will discuss the ten symptoms of organizational change. The process is quite predictable. Then I will suggest a number of requirements for dealing effectively with change. My initial assumption is that all organizations find themselves in flux, today. Sometimes the changes may appear mild, but for the hundreds of dotcoms that have folded and the millions of people who have lost their jobs in the last five years, **dealing with the transitions is tantamount to trying to body surf a tsunami.** In the midst of all this change, which, in some cases, washes away everything that came before, boards of directors and Wall Street analysts have become more and more accustomed to demanding lower costs and higher performance. The street is merciless on those publicly held companies which fail to deliver on predicted earnings.

Given that working hypothesis—and I rarely get an argument about its validity—I will look at what organizations going through transition need. The eight requirements are as clear as the symptoms. Meeting these requirements in a systematic way, paves the way for High Performance.

I will look at the process of attaining High Performance from three discrete but related viewpoints. First, I will examine the five philosophical underpinnings that form the foundation for High Performance. This approach I call the 30,000-foot view. It is high level and big picture. Then we'll drop down 20,000 feet to view specific traits of High Performance that corporate leaders have discussed with me over the last few years. At 10,000 feet, we still have a bird's eye view of the process, but we begin to narrow the focus. Third, I will look at the very specific differences between traditional organizations and a team-based High Performance Culture. Most companies spending money to build teams these days are merely creating groups. That approach is usually just a waste of money! Last, I will outline a plan for taking your organization into the exciting future of High Performance.

This is not a book for organization design practitioners, trainers, or consultants. It is not an academic book designed to train anyone to do anything. I will spare you the usual pedantic review of Open Systems Theory and the General Theory of Organizations. I will have nothing to say about traditional Machine Theory, the Organizational Performance Model, or the Bureaucratic Model of Organizations. You will also be disappointed if you expect a review of either Open Systems Planning or Socio-technical Systems Design.

I promise not to bore you with historical reviews of the theoretical contributions of Max Weber, Frederick W. Taylor, behaviorists like Kurt Lewin, or even modern day theorists like Drucker, Hammer, Blanchard, or Senge. I suppose they are all valuable background reading for some theorist at some B-School, but they offer little practical application for real people leading real businesses. Tom

Peters had his day, but you can only pop so many balloons and shout "Wow" so many times, before the eyes glaze over. You want solutions, not hype and histrionics.

This is also not a book for theorists. I will not discuss homeostatic forces or coded organizational boundaries. None of you have ever seen one, nor has either ever contributed to the bottom line. Along with feedback loops, task core processes, group core processes, and organizational transformational processes, they are the psychobabble of those who have never led a shift, never met a deadline, never handled a union grievance, never cleaned up an environmental spill, never had profit and loss responsibility, and never tried to pacify a real screaming customer. Although the word paradigm might sneak in from time to time, I promise not to use the word "equifinality."

This a book for business leaders who want to create Cultures of High Performance.

You have seen the ads. "Two Days to Top Performance," "Free Your Inner Child," "Transform Your Company with Our Training Specialists," "Personal and Team Mapping," "Building your Learning Organization," "Management Techniques to Revolutionize Your Business," "Nurture Your Inner Child," "Release Your Hidden Giant," "High-Involvement Leadership" (you do this "high involving" on line, by the way) and several others offered by local, national, and international purveyors of mass training. Do these 1-day, 2-day, and 3-day sessions produce anything more than profit for the companies offering the training and seminar business for the local Holiday Inn? Do they create cultures of High Performance or are they merely hype? What is your experience? You signed the checks; what was the return on your investment?

For the last twelve years, our own organizational learnings have increased exponentially. My own company has grown from a personally run sole proprietorship where I was the sole contact, consultant, typist, and trainer, to a corporation of 44 renowned associates who are philosophically and electronically linked around the world. Our learning organization thrives on the ferment of ideas we create as we challenge one another's perceptions and conclusions. The result has been a multi-year conversation about how we can best help companies achieve genuine High Performance.

I owe a debt of gratitude to many companies that have allowed me to work with their leaders and employees over the last thirteen years. I have had a chance to try out bits and pieces of this framework for high performance as the model has evolved over the years. At first the ideas were fledgling and barely took flight. The very diversity of these clients in terms of their businesses, their geography, and the levels of people with whom I have worked, lend great validity to the process I describe here. This book is for you, my clients. Thank you for the constant learnings. Appendix I contains a partial list of credits in twenty-nine countries.

We now know what works and how to help organizations create and sustain a culture of true High Performance.

That is what this book is about. I hope you enjoy it, profit from it, and feel free to challenge it. This conversation is, after all, an ongoing one. High Performance is a work in progress for all of us. You can contact me for my part in the conversation at esipres6@earthlink.net, or by the older POTS at (800) 977-1688.

The world changed, suddenly and dramatically, for the United States on September 11, 2001. The Twin Towers of The World Trade Center were chosen as terrorist targets because they represented the economic heart of the United States and many of the 80 countries that suffered casualties on that day. What was attacked was human and economic freedom and free enterprise itself. The attack was designed to topple our confidence and to force us to question our very way of life.

But, even before militant Islamic terrorists destroyed these symbols of the spirit of capitalism, traditional businesses were in trouble. Expectations were up and profits were down. The boom of the 1990's had collapsed into the tech wreck of the dotcoms. For the business world, the future environment is clear: it is a world of unprecedented danger and volatility. The words "team work" and "high perform-ance" once lip-service-slogans, are now essential to our sur-vival. This is a book for business leaders who want to cre-ate cultures of High Performance during tough times.

CONTENTS

CHAPTER ONE

Greatness or Mediocrity

What is it that makes an organization great? Is it the character of the President or the Chairman of the Board? Is it the long-term market performance of the company's stock? Is it the widespread use of its products? Is it the personality of a Jack Welsh (former General Electric CEO), a Bill Gates (Microsoft), a Steve Case (America Online), a Lou Gerstner (IBM), a Larry Bossidy (Allied Signal), a Norman Schwartzkopf, a Carly Fiorina (Hewlett Packard), a Herb Kelleher (Southwest Airlines), a Phil Condit (Boeing), a Richard Branson (Virgin Airlines), a Colin Powell, or a Ralph Larsen (Johnson & Johnson)? Exactly what is it that makes one company, team, or organization great and widely respected and another merely average or mediocre? Finding the answer to this question has consumed much of our consulting time over the last twelve years.

Regardless of whether we have been asked to mediate conflict, build a more effective senior leadership team, create an innovation pipeline to generate new products, perform an organizational assessment, enhance teamwork, train in diversity, assist in the implementation of SAP or other large system integration, evaluate training and development needs, craft a corporate vision statement, train organizations in e-business, prepare a business strategy, or help to reengineer an entire manufacturing site, the unstated expectation is that we contribute to the creation of an organization with a greater capability to generate High Performance.

Most often, we begin by performing a systematic organizational diagnosis to try to ascertain what is going on that, at present, hinders the attainment of High Performance. We like to supplement such a survey with focus groups in widely scattered geographical regions and interviews with key members of the company. It is a commonplace by now, but it is nonetheless a profound truth—**Every organization is perfectly designed to get the results it gets.** Look at your organization. Do you like what you see? If you do not like the results you see, change the design.

By design, I do not mean to imply simply the way a company has been structured or chooses to go to the marketplace. I am not just talking about whether the company is organized functionally or by strategic business units, whether it is hierarchal in nature or flat and agile, or whether it is matrixed or stove piped. By design I mean the truly essential issues involving motivation, culture, structure, style, vision, and leadership. The requisite constituents of such an organization, quite frankly, have been the focus of professional debate for several years. The wisdom of one age routinely has been called into question by the next. One doctoral dissertation has sought to unseat the thesis of the previous one. Through this healthy Hegelian dialectic, however, we have learned what works and what is merely hype.

Sometimes it is easier to note what does not work. Sending off two or three of your managers, for example, to a Holiday Inn for a one-day, ninety-five-dollar seminar is ludicrous. You can pick up your purchased notebook, fill in the blanks for six hours, and listen to their half hour advertisement for tapes and books, and that's where it will stay—another homogenized seminar checked off on your to do list. The military is infamous for punching their training ticket by sending off their personnel for three hours of in-house, warmed-over TQM or TQL training each week. The training is free to the unit, and it looks as if employees are staying up-to-date with contemporary training. They aren't, of course, but the training schedule is met, the training department looks good, and the training budget can remain emaciated.

Federal and state agencies routinely dumb down the process, as well. They will float a Request for Proposal (RFP), prepared by some in-house training specialist, who wins points with her supervisor by including every jargon-laden phrase of warmed over organizational development (OD) cant for the last ten years, as well as the nine pages of required, but meaningless, bureaucratic requirements. The RFP dictates the content of the training and ensures that no consulting company can innovatively respond to it.

The typical consulting company reviews previous responses to similar projects, gins up fifty pages of boiler plate content, sends it in, says a prayer, and hopes for the best. The companies with the glibbest full time proposal mill will win the majority of the government contracts.

Cost is only one of the selection criteria, the RFP states boldly. Everyone responding to it knows that claim is disingenuous if not an outright lie. But the proposing company slashes its fees to the bare bones and prepares to send their most junior or least qualified people to do the training should they be awarded the contract. Six months later the agency awards the contract to a company that has had a GAO contract for years, a minority or female owned business, or some teacher at a local community college selling his services at $ 400.00 per day. The organization books the training. The requirement is "satisfied." Participants show up disgruntled and leave bored, and nothing changes. What a surprise! You do get what you pay for.

The very process undermines any chance at attaining high performance, creativity, or innovation. The procrustean expectations of the RFP predetermine the mediocre and uncreative responses generated. Every organization is perfectly designed to get the results it gets, and so is every process for getting there. If you want different results, change the process.

You can bring in Career Tracks, SGA, PPD, FTD, DDI, Skill Path, or some other mass training company to fertilize your organization with their off-the- shelf programs and even get a half dozen trainers or human resources personnel "certified" in presenting their programs, but nothing will change. They will simply train you with the same homogenized materials with which they trained six of your competitors. Where's the competitive advantage for you? And, if your executive training budget is flush enough, you can bring in a well-known motivational guru like Tony Robbins or Lou Holtz, or some retired professional football or basketball player to help you release your hidden giant or stroke your inner child.

Well, they can keep their hidden giant, they can baby sit their inner child, and they can keep their canned, off the shelf programs, because they cannot provide the key to generating high performance. You can walk on coals or strip naked in the woods and practice howling with the other hairy beasts, and nothing will change in the boardroom Monday morning.

Creating High Performance demands a systematic approach to changing how you will do business in the future.

It demands High Performance, not Hype.

CHAPTER TWO

New Beginnings

The key word, of course, is "Change." Every one of our corporate clients these days is going through substantial, often gut-wrenching change. Sometimes, the change is a North American company being acquired by a European parent. Sometimes it is a large corporation divesting a less profitable business. Sometimes it is right sizing, down sizing, smart sizing, or otherwise laying off people. Sometimes it is a merger of equals; although, that term is usually just a euphemism for a take over. Sometimes it is change required by shifting technologies, new product orientations, or a conscious shift in business orientation. Sometimes the change requires opening new markets in different cultures. Sometimes the change is a wholesale organizational redesign to delayer, restructure, become more efficient, or overcome the lethargy and inefficiencies of legacy systems. Sometimes it is simply a leader stirring the pot to stimulate creativity and new ideas. Regardless of the reason for the change, it is no fun for the employees forced to endure it.

Nobody likes change, except a wet baby,

but it is the only constant most of our businesses have for the foreseeable future. Change is never easy, but large systems changes have even fewer allies. As early as 1513, a crafty leader named Niccolo lamented his dilemma.

It must be remembered that there is nothing more difficult to plan, more doubtful of success, nor more dangerous to manage than the creation of a new system. For the initiator has the enmity of all who would profit by the preservation of the old institution and merely lukewarm defenders in those who would gain by the new ones.

Machiavelli, *The Prince*

Change implies different problems for different companies. In Crompton Corporation's case, it is the change associated with three name changes in as many years and growth: mergers and acquisitions. For Lockheed Martin, it is the change associated with bringing together dozens of cultures from smaller organizations with diverse cultures and trying to create a coherent corporate culture. For Haworth, it is growing from a U. S. furniture manufacturer to a global business in less than ten years. Change for Agfa Corporation involves getting spun off from German Bayer Corporation, changing leadership from a German to a Finn, and then dealing with a new Belgian leadership team flexing its muscle from Mortsel, Belgium. For Sterling Diagnostics, change meant getting divested from DuPont de Nemours and then getting sold to the Belgians who said "cut cost, cut cost, cut cost."

Change for Lucent Technologies is an ongoing effort to recover from the rapid decline from its glory days of $ 86 / share stock price during the peak of the e-business glut to the $ 6 / share of 2001 and talk of bankruptcy. Change for Pfizer means trying to incorporate Warner Lambert into its existing value structure. Change for PNC means creating new profitability by moving away from traditional banking revenue generation to a new pay for services model, and change for Bayer Diagnostics means ongoing work with the Chiron acquisition. Change for Ford Motor Company means paying massive settlements for overturned Explorers, severing all ties with Firestone, and suing its former long-standing business partner. Change for Bristol-Myers Squibb means accommodating the acquisition of DuPont's pharmaceutical business.

Change for the United States Army means shifting its focus in 2001 from being "all that you can be," a slogan that challenged everyone to constant improvement, to the marketing hype and Narcissism of each soldier's becoming an "Army of One." And, at the same time the army shifted its public focus from teamwork to individualism, it stripped the Special Forces (you would call them the Green Berets) and Rangers from their prized and unique berets and gave them to everyone in the army. So much for esprit de corps! The dumbing down of our culture has migrated from the public schools to the battlefield and the Pentagon. Change for most of the rest of you means, if nothing else, cut costs and reduce heads. Those who are left are expected to do more with less.

Change can be as civilization shattering as the September eleventh terrorist attack on the United States, as fundamental to business as Jürgen Dormann, Chairman of Hoechst, AG, announcing in *Chemical Week* that the future of the German chemical giant would be "pharmaceuticals, pharmaceuticals, pharmaceuticals," as financially devastating as Eli Lilly's losing patent protection for some of its major drugs, as tepid as Medrad's launching a new innovation initiative, or as uninspiring as Coca Cola announcing it was adding lemon to its new Diet Coke. Yuk! Whenever the change is announced, employees, and occasionally consumers, have been conditioned to ask, "What am I about to lose this time?"

CHAPTER THREE

Carnack, the Magnificent, Sees All

Despite the uneasy nature of change, the good news is that its symptoms are as predictable as the measles, and for that reason its treatment is also reasonably simple in concept, just difficult to implement. Think about the changes underway in your business right now. Put yourself in the shoes of your employees. How do they feel? What are their expectations? What feedback do you get or do you give to those in charge? Are we having fun, yet?

Symptom I: A Sense of Uncertainty

If you are experiencing changes in your job, business, or market, one of the first symptoms you will recognize throughout your organization is a sense of uncertainty, lack of stability, or outright fear. People just do not know what to expect. Last year the company reduced headcount by 3500 and shut down one division; who knows what is going to happen this year. There are rumors of a merger. Do I trade the car in for a new one? Do I buy that house I've been looking at? Will the money be there when I need it? What happens to my medical benefits? My husband needs major surgery, and my oldest daughter is a junior in college. The company has reorganized three times in the last five years, and now we are introducing SAP across the organization. How will that impact my job in customer service? There is white powder on the mailroom floor. Is it the result of a shoddy cleaning service or the sign of an anthrax attack by terrorists?

After Lucent Technologies sliced 15,000 permanent heads in the year 2000 and another 5500 contract employees in 2001, paranoia became rampant. The stock was in a free fall, and all the employees were convinced there would be another massive head count reduction in the near future, or a foreign acquisition; that is, if the company survived at all. When the French decided the acquisition was off, the employees were not at all surprised to hear of another 20,000-person reduction in July of 2001. Here is a company known from its inception for hiring only the very best people that, by consensus, had a predictably great future, which, because of management miscues, bloated costs, and a vacuum of visionary leadership, hit the endangered companies list. Wisely, everyone with a future has had a resume on the street for three years, and the half of Lucent employees who remain are predicting the worst as the company prepares to "go it alone," according to the chairman, for the indefinite future.

Company loyalty, which, in the good old days, many organizations fostered and most employees counted on, is gone. The concept is bankrupt. Just add up the corporate body count over the last ten years, even from some very paternalistic companies known for caring about their employees, Kodak, DuPont, IBM, General Electric, Sears, Nabisco, Hoechst, Heinz, Proctor and Gamble, and many others, and you realize the first thing any company does these days to cut costs is to reduce headcount. When I wrote *Taming the Scorpion: Preparing Business for the Third Millennium,* I tried to document in one of the chapters all the major reductions that had been announced in the previous two years. The most frustrating task I had was every time I went back to proof read the text or work on a new chapter, there had been 12,000 more here and 13,000 more there, and 5000 more in another company. Even when reading every business journal I could find and reviewing most major annual reports, I could not stay up with the head count reductions taking place within the Fortune 500 community.

Employees ask the appropriate question: if "they" have no loyalty to me, why should I be loyal to them? It is a fair question. Consequently, headhunters have a lucrative field day, and most managers and executives I talk with these days have a current active resume.

Everyone is in play all the time.

Symptom II: Poor Information

The quality of information received during times of transition is also indicative of the changes occurring. Employees will see any information provided as being poor in quality. What is said on Monday will change by Friday. Announcements from the leadership team in March are called into question by the cafeteria rumors in May. Every time a new person shows up wearing a suit out on the production floor, employees will be convinced someone is doing another due diligence. Often, because studies are underway, or McKinsey is doing the strategy, or a major reengineering effort is underway, there is not a lot that can be communicated, without violating confidences. The result is that very little is communicated, and employees become suspicious.

Rule number one of organizational communication is that,

When no information is communicated, people will invent it.

The corollary to rule number one is that the information created is negative in direct proportion to the amount created. In other words, communicate or suffer the consequences.

Symptom III: Inconsistent Leaders

The consequence of Symptoms I & II is that employees will perceive those leading the change process as inconsistent, at best, and incompetent, at worst. The conversation at the water fountain and at the smoke shack centers on the inability of the senior leadership to set a vision, to lead the company through the miasma that exists. Of course the employees don't use this language. Usually, what they say, is their bosses obviously don't know their #%$@* from a hole in the ground. But the sentiment is the same.

In one company I was working with recently, the employees had convinced themselves that the plant leadership team was being paid a bonus by the company for every employee they could lay off. Furthermore, convinced that their plant was going to be shut down, they began the rumor that the company was buying property in a different state and had already made a down payment on the property. It took one telephone call at lunchtime to dismantle the rumor. Now, why did I have to do that? Where was the leadership team? Why didn't the plant management know that was a concern?

Too often the leadership team is so busy fighting alligators from the outside during times of change they are unaware of major issues that seek to undo them internally. When the leadership team is not engaged and communicating frequently, employees will perceive senior managers as just reacting to the changes coming down the line rather than effectively setting an agenda to lead the change. As a consequence of the first three symptoms, we get number four.

Symptom IV: More Control
Employees start demanding more control. Here is the irony. For years, employees at most levels of the organization have lobbied for more freedom. "Let us have more involvement! Why can't we have a small business mentality and make more decisions locally? Let us act more entrepreneurially! Why do you micromanage us and direct our every activity? Listen to us and give us more input to the decision-making process! Why do you control us so tightly?"

Now, the same people because of the flux, the fear, the inconsistency, and the poor information start demanding, "Look! Just tell us our job! What do you want us to do by Friday?" Frustrated by their inability to influence decisions swirling around them, fearful of the changes taking place, and frustrated by not getting answers to their question, employees get mentally myopic and become victims in their own minds merely capable of responding to simple directives. The victim mentality enervates employees and sucks the life out of High Performance.

Symptom V: Emotional Stress

As a result, employees and those around them experience high levels of emotional stress. And, stress kills. Not always, of course, but sometimes. What you will notice, however, as symptoms of stress, are more job-related illnesses. Employees are sick more often. People are out on disability more frequently and for longer periods of time. Even in work places where safety is the number one priority—and I come from the school of thought that says that every accident is 100% preventable—near misses occur more frequently. Often they go unreported and safety violations begin to occur. When every employee is worried whether or not she or he will be the next one to go, even reporting a near miss becomes a potentially career threatening move.

Where change is rampant, we find higher levels of family discord, spousal and child abuse cases become more frequent, and the Jack Daniels is harder to find on the shelves of the state liquor store. Indeed, all the classic symptoms of societal decay occur at higher levels: alcoholism, drug use, family dissolution, and physical abuse. Welcome to the world of organizational change.

Thus, organizations going through such changes need to be put on notice that they have special moral obligations to train more frequently and to make counseling services easily accessible to those who may need help. In the last year alone, I personally know of six people in five different corporations on the east coast, within the last year, who committed suicide because of events directly related to job loss and organizational change. There are probably many more. Employees come to feel out of control with no capability of influencing events swirling around them. We have known for years that this loss of control can be deadly.

Back during the cold war period, the Soviets performed a number of experiments in control to try to understand the consequences of the loss of control on individuals' ability to function. One such experiment involved seven pairs of Hamadryas baboons. Now, Hamadryas baboons, I am told, unlike human beings, mate for life. So the nasty Soviets (remember, we hated them back then) took these seven pairs of Hamadryas baboons, which had been living in connubial bliss for several years, and separated them into fourteen separate cages—nasty Soviets! They put the seven female baboons on one side of the lab and the seven male baboons on the other side of the lab, just fourteen feet away. Into the cages with the original seven female baboons, they introduced seven new male baboon partners, just to see what would happen.

Inside of seven months, all the original male baboons were dead, from heart attack, stroke, and high blood pressure. What's the only thing that changed? The Soviets, pragmatists that they are, said fourteen feet. For our purposes, the only thing that changed was that the seven original male baboons had no control over what they saw happening just fourteen feet away. Think of your employees watching all the changes taking place around them, changes often dictated from Germany, Switzerland, Belgium, Great Britain, Japan, France, or a headquarters in some location far removed from their site, changes over which they have no control. Stress kills!

Symptom VI: Undirected High Energy
In the distant hypothesized past, when Mukluk, our ancient, hairy, Cro-Magnon relative, was facing the Tyrannosaurus Rex determining which of them would be supper for the other, adrenalin was useful to prompt the fight or flight syndrome. Today, when the beasts are smaller and some of us are less hairy, the adrenalin is more dangerous. With no place to run, we fight saber tooth tigers inside on a daily basis. During these times of stress, the adrenalin says DO SOMETHING! One way we humans have learned to purge all the adrenalin we pump into our system during times of stress, then, is to do something. We

demonstrate high energy, often undirected, and **just do something.**

One real tribute to the professionalism of the Bush administration and his senior foreign policy team in Washington D. C. is the lack of immediate response after the attack of 911. They did not "just do something" (launch a missile, drop a bomb, or take out an aspirin factory in some foreign country) despite the saber rattling and jingoism of even liberal news media. They took time and acted deliberately; they built an international coalition and established a global agenda for including the Moslem world in a unified attack on terrorism. Their energy was directed and focused.

Look at all the trivial projects that get started in your company during times of stress or change that have no contribution to the problems the organization is actually facing. At home, some individuals under stress clean furiously, dig in the garden, rearrange the closets, iron until their arm hurts, or re-alphabetize the spice shelf. My mother used to wash clothes by hand into the wee hours of the morning. Others go outside and shoot hoops into the dark or weed whack themselves into relative calm. At work, we write up huge "do lists," schedule meaningless meetings, issue Franklin Planners to everybody, schedule time management classes, and sanction one meaningless project after the other. Better to be doing something, anything, than feel out of control. We rearrange the deck chairs on the *Titanic* while the violins play "Nearer My God to Thee."

Symptom VII: Increased Conflict
Because of all the kinetic energy and running about, it is almost inevitable that we start bumping into one another, and we get increased conflict, particularly between intact groups. Groups, shifts, unions, and teams, which in the past have cooperated with one another, suddenly find themselves at odds on a daily basis. "It's their fault" becomes the new organizational mantra. There are more yelling matches at home and more dissatisfaction and unrest in the workplace.

When the future is uncertain, human beings seek out the company of those they trust most. Those they trust tend to be those they know best—those in their work group. They circle the wagons and see all those outside their closed circle as potential enemies. Organizational paranoia spreads like wild fire. "Maybe, if we link arms, and keep the others out, when the next reduction occurs, it will be in their group not ours." Conflict becomes almost inevitable.

Symptom VIII: An Epidemic of Blame

The natural consequence is that blaming becomes epidemic. It is not an enjoyable place to work any more. No one accepts criticism gracefully. No one wants any suggestions. Everyone believes they are working harder than everyone else. You come home stressed out, tired, and ready to share your frustration with the family. It is harder than ever to keep Tylenol in the medicine cabinet, and that blood pressure medication your doctor suggested during your last physical looks really attractive. Since the workplace of the present is so bad, there appears to be only one alternative.

Symptom IX: Reverence for the Past

Can't we just bring back the old Coke? No one asked the company to change. We start revering past patterns of behavior. They were the "Good Old Days." At home, the step kids look to the old family, the missing dad, the missing mom as the good old days. They have forgotten the yelling, the doors slamming, and the rampant meanness. On the job, we look to our previous owners and former presidents. Remember when our company was owned by Dow Corning, Compugraphics, Uniroyal, Digital, AT&T, Warner Lambert, or Harris Chemical? Remember when... was the chairman? Remember when we were organized by...? They were the Good Old Days!

Well, the truth is that they weren't! But today it just seems that way. This might not be a comforting thought, but

five years from now.... Today will be the good old days.

It's a scary thought isn't it?

Symptom X: Anger Directed at Those in Charge

Because of all this—because of the first nine symptoms—anger will be directed at those leading the change process—you. But that is why you are paid so handsomely. Some of these symptoms may not exist in your organization, but we routinely see most of them when organizations undergo significant transitions. How does your business score?

SYMPTOM REVIEW

I. High uncertainty	yes	no
II. Poor, inadequate information	yes	no
III. Inconsistent leadership	yes	no
IV. Desire for control	yes	no
V. Emotional stress	yes	no
VI. Spasmodic, undirected energy	yes	no
VII. Increased conflict	yes	no
VIII. An epidemic of blame	yes	no
IX. Bring back the old Coke	yes	no
X. Anger directed at those in charge.	yes	no

If you have five or more responses in the "yes" column, seek outside help immediately!

CHAPTER FOUR

The Doctor is In

So far we have only dealt with the easy stuff. Identifying the symptoms is fairly easy. It's is like going to the doctor, pointing to your stomach, and saying, "it hurts here." You know it hurts. What you want to know is how to fix it. You want the doctor to say "Mylanta." So, if you score mostly in the "yes" column, above, the question is, what are you going to do about it? Fortunately, the cure is as prescribable as the symptoms are predictable. There are certain things that every organization undergoing transitions needs.

Requirement I: Leaders Capable of Declaring a Clear and Compelling Case for Change.
Let's take it piece by piece. First of all "leaders." There are leaders and there are managers. Any of us can learn to act like the other—each has a specific cognitive skill set—but given our personalities, our natural preferences, we have a natural predilection for one over the other. Management texts seem to shift back and forth over the years praising first one then the other. John Kotter brought some sanity to the discussion with his book, *A Force For Change*. The subtitle is perhaps more important than the title for our purposes: "How Leadership Differs From Management."

Kotter's thesis is clear. Managers do some things, and leaders do other things. Leaders spend the bulk of their time setting direction, visioning, aligning others, communicating, and inspiring. Managers, on the other hand, spend their efforts planning, budgeting, setting intermediate targets, organizing, staffing, delegating, and controlling. They each spend time solving problems, but they do it from different vantage points. Leaders foster change, and managers try to establish procedures and processes that encourage predictability. This is not earth shattering information, but I'd wager, if you survey your own intellectual capital, you will agree that one of these skill sets comes easier to you than the other. It is not that one is good and the other is bad. The point is that while both are critical for business success, it is difficult to master each.

I remember, after a playoff game between the Indianapolis Colts and the New England Patriots, hearing Peyton Manning describe what a leader does. For those of you who are not fans of professional football, Peyton is the son of Archie Manning (himself a great quarterback) and the quarterback for the Indianapolis Colts—a team with which I spend a good bit of time. His comments are at Appendix III. As fans watch Manning on the field, walking up and down the offensive line, shouting and gesticulating, there is no doubt in anyone's mind who is in charge. He is the on-field leader! What I find interesting about his description of a leader is that of the twenty things he has to do between breaking the huddle (launching your company's strategic plan) and running the play—what he calls DETONA-TION (you might call it achieving business success)—only five concern his own organization. The other fifteen concern the competition and the marketplace. I dare say most ineffective business leaders, those who think they are over-worked and misunderstood, reverse the proportion.

While the skill sets of both leaders and managers are neces-sary, some jobs require one skill set far more than the other. Just as a leader like Patton would never have suc-ceeded managing Sears, so most CEOs couldn't hack it in combat. You can't manage soldiers into battle. McNamara tried it, and it was a debacle for which he is still apologiz-ing. The two skill sets are fairly discrete. At different stages of the business cycle, one skill set may be more important than the other. During times of change we need "leaders," people who will set the agenda, who will see the future and make the "invisible" visible for others. These men and women will align teams and people, and business partners with clear strategies for attaining the vision.

During times of change, organizations need leaders who will lead proactively and not wait for circumstances to dictate their future course.

One practical way leaders can begin this process is to seek out "killer phrases" that undermine change and thwart innovative ideas and eliminate them. You have heard many of them:

1. The lawyers won't allow it.
2. You can't do that in the South.
3. We tried that before.
4. The analysts won't like it.
5. Hey, this is New England.
6. It's too risky.
7. If it's not broke, don't fix it.
8. If I want your opinion, I'll give it to you!
9. The Germans will never agree to that!

You can probably fill in the one your company is famous for trotting out during times of change. Often we talk ourselves out of changes before we even consider them.

The second part of the statement takes us to the kind of leader required. It is one capable of declaring a clear and compelling case for change, what some consultants call a "burning platform." My limo driver in Norfolk, Virginia used to regale me with stories about his glory days as an explosives expert on the oilrigs off Louisiana during the boom times (no pun intended). Let's go to one of his rigs. It is a balmy June afternoon, the temperature is about 85 degrees, and you are a pipe fitter working about nine stories above the deck. You are watching the dolphins jump out of the beautiful blue sea, the gulls and terns are squawking as they dive into the schools of tiny mackerel, and someone shouts at you to JUMP. You are likely to ask... What? "Why?" It makes no sense. The status quo is just fine.

But let's go back to that same rig. You are on the ninth story fixing some cables. You smell smoke and look down to see flames spreading over the deck. The thick black smoke is billowing up toward you. Explosions echo off the metal below. Fifty-five gallon drums are blowing off the deck in all directions. When someone shouts "Jump," you are not going to hear him are you? No, you've already jumped. It is amazing what incentive a burning platform can give you. The leader's task is to create the burning platform in order to provide employees with the reason for change.

**Good people respond well to change.
Exceptional people create the changes.**

Too often organizational leaders begin major change initiatives without creating the burning platform—without creating the compelling reason for change. We need to cut costs; we need to cut heads; we need to introduce SAP. We are going to reorganize from a functional organization to strategic business units; we are implementing self-managed work teams across all of manufacturing. If this is all the company hears, the natural response is, "why?" Sometimes leaders assume everyone will be on board simply because they have spoken. Not a chance. Even if the employees are willing to do just as they are ordered, you need them motivated and understanding the process to generate High Performance. It is a leadership task to create the compelling reason to change. This may require that we explain our business model, discuss the competition, explain our marketing approach. In short, it demands that we instill a business sense in our employees.

**The failure to instill this business sense in employees
at every level of the organization may be the single
greatest down fall of businesses today.**

Requirement II: A Widely Publicized Vision of What the Future will be.

At Ford, quality is... job one. Now, this may be absolute nonsense, and some of the events surrounding Ford's defunct partnership with Firestone suggests it is, but the important point is that not only does everyone at Ford know this phrase, but so do you! It is part of Ford's vision, and it has been so well communicated and widely publicized, it has also become part of our culture. Many years ago, a great prophet warned us: "without a vision, the people perish." He was right then, and he is still right. A vision, as we discussed earlier, is a powerful business principle. Too often it is not done right! Let's discuss one case where it was.

His name is G. W. Haworth. He was a high school shop teacher who had a vision to make furniture. After being turned down for business loans by most of the banks in and around Holland, Michigan, his parents gave him their life savings. He reluctantly used their ten thousand dollars and began a Horatio Alger success story that grew into a multi hundred million dollar business rivaling Steelcase, Inc. for market leadership in high-end office furniture. I met him through my colleague, Judith, who was working with the Human Resources Vice President on a series of organizational issues. In the early 1990's the company's leadership decided they wanted to create a global business that would grow into a one billion dollar business by the year 2005.

As we talked with each member of the senior business team, it became clear they had tremendous talent but lacked the collective vision to pull it off. We suggested that if they wanted a global business they should not hold their upcoming leadership conference in Holland, Michigan; they should use the conference to make a global statement. They had recently purchased an Italian company called Castelli Spa in Bologna, Italy. The company's leadership wisely made the decision to go there for their Global Visioning Conference. That decision was the first of many that led them to create a successful vision. The next decision had to do with identifying who would attend. Would they take their leadership team to create the vision and then have to spend the next 5 years trying to get the company to buy in, or was there a riskier and more expensive, but more logical and potentially more profitable alternative?

With our encouragement, they chose the alternative. They took dozens of supervisors, fore persons, hourly operators, cabinetmakers, and wood workers from Holland, Michigan along with their senior leaders to Bologna, Italy. They also invited senior sales and marketing people from North America and Europe, heads of businesses they had recently acquired from several countries, and leaders of a dozen or more of their major customers from around the world. For four days, in several languages, we created a global vision that would take the company into the future. It was hardly a boondoggle or "European Vacation" for those selected to attend. There was a lot of preparatory work from all the employees in the company before the conference, a lot of hard work at the conference by over one hundred people speaking several different languages, and a lot of follow-up work after the conference. The result? The company has doubled in size since the conference and achieved the one billion dollar goal six years early. This level of involvement is not always necessary, but it was for this company in this industry.

A vision developed well, compels business success.

But let's say you are not so fortunate. You do not work in a company with visionary leaders. In fact they think having a vision is silly. You might also work in a company that has a vision, but, quite frankly, it stinks and was badly developed by uncreative people. What do you do? You must have a vision, so you create one for your division, your business unit, or your team. In short, you cannot allow your organization to be handicapped by a void in leadership at the top of your organization. You act and lead from where you are. Can you still be successful without leadership from the top? No ship has a rudder at the front. As canvas sailors know, you can turn a big boat with a clever hand on the rudder at the stern. It just may take more tact. Trickle up leadership can sometimes be more powerful than its better-known trickle down relative.

Requirement III. There must be a plan for managing the transition.
Here is the chance for those with a natural preference for

management skills to come to the forefront to create a clear plan with PPR's, specific timelines, and deadlines that include roles, activities, and means of accountability. This plan probably begins with a formal current state assessment that measures where the company is now on a series of behavior-based performance variables and then builds a plan to get where the vision needs to be.

A vision without a plan is valueless.

Understanding roles and having clearly defined responsibilities and reporting requirements take on added importance during times of major change. Too often people are shifted around and moved into new jobs when major changes occur without adequate preparation for the assignment. Because of seniority or some other job saving HR policy, those who have worked 9am-5pm for years suddenly find themselves pulling shift just to have a job. Those who used to work in R&D before the Europeans shut down all R&D in the States and moved it all to Frankfurt or Mortsel or Leverkusen, or Liverpool, now find themselves pulling shift duty in Manufacturing or performing checks in Quality Assurance.

Whereas, in the past, people would have been trained in their job for days, if not weeks, now employees find themselves thrust into roles with little preparation for the tasks required or even in the safety requirements for the job. In many cases employees do not really know what the job entails, for what they are being held responsible, and to whom they report. No wonder, then, that the quality slips, safety seems neglected, and the chain of command seems to be in disarray.

It is during times of change that organizations also need to stop paying people just for "showing up." Often organizations have slipped unconsciously into the habit of simply paying people because they show up to work for x number of days per year. Employees have developed the entitlement mentality.

The time of change is the time to kill the entitlement mentality.

Requirement IV. Structures for Managing the Change.
Remember your last trip to New York City or Chicago or Atlanta or Los Angeles? Remember all those skyscrapers being repointed, having the facades refurbished, or being completely redesigned? The scaffolding covered the entire building and stayed there for months if not years in the case of larger buildings. If you had to walk past one of these buildings, there were artificial tunnels created so you could pass by without concrete or rebar falling on your head. It almost looked like the construction scaffolding was part of the permanent structure. Then, suddenly, on your fifth trip back, the scaffolding was gone; you could walk on the sidewalk again, and the building looked brand new.

Routinely, during times of significant change, organizations need to construct temporary structures that will assist the company in its changes but which may go away when the change is complete. To the employees, for all intents and purposes, they would swear the structure they are looking at is permanent; then, suddenly, it is gone and the organization looks brand new.

One of our clients, recently acquired by a European company, was being repeatedly directed to make significant reductions in cost. The R&D building was shut down and all employees let go or reassigned to manufacturing. The plant management shut down the cafeteria to save money, and stringent cost cutting measures were put into place: lights were turned off, utilities were turned down, and fax machines and copiers were eliminated. The construction company, which for years had maintained a large presence on the site, had its contract cancelled, and all training ceased. Headcount on the site was reduced from 1500 to 550 in less than one year, and several major products, once manufactured on the site, were sent back to Europe to be manufactured there. The employees were certain the plant would close within the year.

We were invited in by the site management team to help these 550 remaining employees deal with the changes associated with these transitions. When my senior associate and I showed up at the first session, we began by asking the attendees to tell us about the changes they had experienced over the last two years. There was dead silence. We tried a couple more times to solicit feedback from the participants in the session but had little success. Finally, someone raised his hand and said, "OK, Bill, we all know why you and Leah are here. The company's management know that we trust you, so they have hired you two to make us feel good so we will work harder and harder until they shut us down." That was not true, and there was no plan to shut the site down, but it did little good, at the time, to try to persuade them differently. It was just their perception, but perception is reality.

The question remains, is this changing structure temporary or permanent? On this site, the jury may still be out on the longevity of the business, but not infrequently, these measures are temporary. At this site, because of hard work, sacrifice, and ingenuity, the employees were able to reduce the cost per pound of product to the lowest of all the other geographical sites in the company. From the plant management's perspective, the changes made were keeping the plant open. Will those changes be enough for the European ownership to keep a U. S. manufacturing presence? It is an open question. Two years later the company may well be adding headcount, reintroducing products, and opening new production lines. If the structures are temporary, say so. If they are permanent, say so!

Requirement V. Resources to Support the Transition.
Most people in the consulting and training business know that a general business decline, a weak market, impacts their businesses first. If a company has to reduce costs, the first thing to go is training. It always happens. First, the company cancels or postpones all training and consulting from the outside; team building ceases. The diversity initiative is put on hold. The president or COO takes a personal interest in all consultants being employed by the business

groups and sometimes demands sole approval authority for hiring a consultant at about the same time the company slashes the travel budget and cuts out all business class travel across the big or little pond, except for the EVP's. If a megalomaniac leads your company, you also start washing light bulbs, and you cancel the company picnic and quality day as well as the holiday party. Internally you perform an audit of all training needs and pare back the training staff or eliminate it altogether.

These actions merely serve as harbingers of the end for employees who knew the company was in trouble and that more changes for the company, always hyped in glowing terms by the president, merely meant the employees would be losing more. Meanwhile, the employees will learn about every senior executive perk not being cut and recognize that they are the only ones paying the price.

Smart, high performing companies know that the time to train is when the company is going through its greatest changes.

A couple years back, our firm worked with a company in the high desert of California that had experienced major personnel cutbacks and business decline. The number of employees had been reduced from 3000 to 800. One visionary safety manager recognized the seeds of destruction that had been sewn by shortsighted leadership and asked us to present two days of training for all employees. We spent one day working with the results of the Myers-Briggs Type Indicator® and behavioral consequences of personality preferences using Temperament Theory and one day immersing employees in an interactive manufacturing simulation called the Flying Starship Factory. We spent the last hour of the second day looking at fourteen differences between traditional workplaces and truly High Performing Teams. The senior management at the company headquarters tried to shut the training down because it was costing training money, but the safety manager risked his career by continuing to champion the process. The results were extraordinary. Morale improved instantaneously, cooperation between the three physical sites gradually improved, productivity increased, costs were reduced across the board because employees took ownership for reining in costs in their particular areas of responsibility, and the employees loved it and asked for more. It sometimes takes **one** value-centered leader, willing to risk it all, to change the culture.

I was recently working with a manufacturing site in North Carolina. It had been through two acquisitions and corporate name changes in the previous three years. Five years earlier, the plant had been part of a large division in part of a large Fortune 100 Company. Money was no object. Customers were plentiful. The plant was situated on a beautiful piece of hilly terrain with waterfalls and wild life running abundantly. There was a large stocked lake and picnic facilities for the families of the employees. The corporation would often bring key customers to the site to entertain them. Those who worked on the site were proud of their company and delighted to be part of a company that fostered a family atmosphere.

Then, suddenly, the market changed. New technologies impacted their traditional products; they were divested and picked up by a company that milked the cow until it was nearly dry. Next, a small, multinational corporation with a corporate headquarters situated across the Atlantic Ocean and a U. S. headquarters located five states away acquired the business. The plant's headcount had been halved over the prior two years, and more reductions were forthcoming. No one had announced the specific numbers yet to the employees, but the check out clerks at the local K-Mart seemed to know, down to the person, how many would be going. Costs were cut dramatically in an effort to please the new masters; buildings were closed and services to the employees were reduced. Profit sharing ended, and new retirement and medical plans were introduced. Most of the employees knew that they worked for the best company within a hundred miles. There were no other viable job options in the area, and those companies present were also going through major shakeups and reductions.

The employees were hurt, angry, suspicious, fearful, and full of blame for those who ran the plant as well as for the company which had acquired them. It did little good to tell them that if they had not been acquired and forced to go through all the changes that had occurred over the previous two years, that the doors would have been shut a year earlier. The market had simply changed around them.

Prior to some of the major cuts, the acquiring corporation had extended its diversity initiative to the site. That was a gutsy move by a sharp Human Resources Vice President who knew that valuing diversity was a prudent business issue, and she wanted the new site to know right from the start that diversity of thought, perceptions, race, gender, and judgment were critical for business success. I had also met the site manager a year earlier during this training and at an off site team building session sponsored by the vice president of manufacturing, and knew him to be a person of integrity who cared greatly about the site, his friends who worked there, and the impact the site had on the small local community. He had also surrounded himself with a management staff, which shared his concern for the people being impacted as well as his desire to make the site profitable. They knew they could succeed in meeting the corporate demands for cost, quality, and production, if they could just get a modicum of support from Europe and if they could reengage their employees.

Despite criticism from the new owners, complaints from business directors, and misgivings expressed by the new North American President, the site manager took his team off site for 2½ days, and we developed a strategy for reengaging the employees. The management team decided they would sponsor a day of training for all 600 employees remaining on the site on dealing with a changing workplace and their responsibilities to readjust their thinking about the nature of work and jobs in the third millennium. We presented the training in groups of no more than 30 persons per session, with two of our consultants present in each session.

I had warned the plant manager going in that he and his staff would be criticized for spending money for training when all they heard was the imperative to cut costs. Furthermore, I suggested, even the employees left employed on the site would criticize the plant management for spending money for training when many of them had lost friends and family members due to job cuts. We were not disappointed in our expectations. The plant manager got it from all sides. He was roundly criticized; meanwhile, he helped his employees adjust to the changes swirling around them, helped them understand the nature of the business and how the market place had changed, and how their learning about the changing nature of work in the third millennium would benefit them in their current jobs and wherever they might work in the future.

Smart, high performing business leaders know that the time to dedicate resources—people, money, technology, time, and training—is when the greatest changes are occurring.

The company must make people available for training, dedicate funds for the training, and allocate time for the training. The critical time to motivate, inspire, and redirect employee energy through training is when monumental change is expected. Unfortunately, that is the time when most shortsighted companies cut training funds and limit the use of outside consultants.

Requirement VI: Effective Communication.
This point seems obvious. We all claim to value it, but very few of us do it. Often the reason is outright fear: fear of hurting someone, fear of censure, fear of criticism. Effective communication means understanding the difference between making announcements and providing high quality information. It means providing mechanisms for ongoing feedback from and between all levels of the organization.

During times of change, people crave attention and information. When they are not being communicated with on a frequent basis they will assume they are being kept in the dark purposely, and, as I mentioned earlier, they will assume the worst. Regularly-scheduled town meetings, weekly e-mails, personal notes, closed circuit TV presentations, flipcharts out on the floor, lunching with small groups of five to ten employees at a time are all effective—even if there is nothing to communicate. Nothing beats the boss just walking through the area and saying hello at 2 pm and 3 am. Just being there, without a message to deliver, counts for a lot.

During times of change, your full time job is leading and managing the change process, and, oh yes, it is always a time of change.

Requirement VII. Political Savvy.

This consideration is a vital one in heavily matrixed organizations, companies with dual or multiple reporting roles, and those with parent companies distantly removed. Times of change demand that we pay careful attention to existing organizational power dynamics. Most business leaders boast to me that theirs is not a political organization. "I won't tolerate politics being played, Jeffries. I weed it out!" It is a pompous, self-serving assertion. Every company I know has its politics being played every day. Smart companies admit it, try to limit it, and learn how to leverage it for their advantage.

I am a powerboat sailor. When I go out onto the Chesapeake Bay fishing for blues or take my daughter water skiing off the beach at Ocean City, New Jersey I like about 400 HP behind my boat. I can turn on a dime and stick the bow straight into a twenty-knot gale and make for homeport with the waves breaking over my bow. That's fun for me, and it doesn't take a lot of finesse, to pull it off. My wife is a canvass sailor. She knows my approach to sailing won't work with her J-boat or catamaran. She has to tact and jibe to get us across the gulf off the coast of Longboat Key, Florida. Successfully dealing with organizational power dynamics in complex organizations requires her skilled hand on the tiller, not my forward assault. Tact is imperative.

During times of change, organizational leaders need to pay close attention to who is in and who is out. They need to be aware of the vested interests of division leaders, business directors, chief stewards, international union representatives, and other organizational power brokers. They need to understand how the analysts on Wall Street or in Brussels, London, or Tokyo are viewing their potential. They need to seek out champions at all levels of the organization who can assist them. And they need to find champions outside the organization who have contacts that can assist them in surviving the changes underway.

Organizational change sometimes is like guerrilla warfare at its most basic level. Mao was right about the need to win the hearts and minds of the people. Nowhere is this truer then when change is underway. An old, wrinkled Laotian warrior one time passed on some wisdom to me that has stood me in good stead a number of times:

"Only the most foolish of mice," he said, "would hide in a cat's ear. But only the wisest of cats would look there for the mouse."

During times of significant change, savvy mice can become true allies in highly politicized organizations.

Requirement VIII. Islands of Stability.

When those "times, they are a changing" it is vital to know what you can count on to remain constant. People need stability in times of flux. Sometimes, that's all employees ask for. Leaders need to be able to declare, "look, a lot is going to change in the coming months and years, even I don't know all the changes that will occur. But, amid all the changes, the following three things, or four things, or five things WILL NOT CHANGE." Leaders must be clear about what is changing and what is remaining stable. Even Indiana Jones, as he charged across fiery lakes and snake-infested swamps, had occasional rocks that never moved. They were his steppingstones to success. It was Dr. Jones' task to crack the code and figure out what was stable in his world and what might be subject to change. Likewise, leaders must figure out what some islands of stability are on which employees can depend. Those islands might include a guarantee from the plant manager or senior business director that:

1. no layoffs will occur without X months notice,
2. safety will remain our number one priority at all times,
3. once the senior team has decided on production changes, we will inform you within 24 hours, or
4. although some jobs may be lost due to retirement packages offered, no jobs will be cut because of our reengineering plan.
5. we will not attempt to decertify the union.

Let's review these 8 Requirements:

Requirements for Organizations Undergoing Transition

I. Leaders capable of declaring a compelling case for change

II. Widely publicized vision

III. Detailed transition plan

IV. Structures for managing the transition

V. Resources to support the transition

VI. Effective communication

VII. Political savvy

VIII. Islands of stability

Are you up to the task? This is the nature of the changing world. Creating a culture of high performance begins by recognizing the nature of change, how it impacts the organization, and what the organization needs to guide it though.

CHAPTER FIVE

The View From 30,000 Feet

Last Father's Day I was sitting in our back yard with my five-year old son, Paul, watching the waterfall that goes from the vanishing edge of the swimming pool, down a fifteen foot waterfall where it cascades into the retention pond before being circulated back up into the pool. Below that pond another waterfall runs thirty feet into a small stream at the base of a hill. The whole area is surrounded by hundred-year-old trees, giant smoky sycamores, and flowering shrubs of all varieties. It is my favorite place to write and one of my young son's favorite places to play.

Paul said, "you know Dad, sometimes life is confusing." I knew he had a profound learning underway so I pursued the thought. "Why is that?" I probed. "Well, Dad, when I am in the swimming pool it looks like I am going to float over the edge into the tree tops, and I can't see the water flowing down to the stream. It is like it doesn't exist. When I stand in the waterfall, I can't see the pool, I can't see the waterfall, but I hear it. When I stand in the stream, I see the huge stone wall bigger than Shrek along the pool, but I really don't see the waterfall or the pool. Which one of these pictures is real?" This is not an unusual conversation in my home, so I put on my best Solomonic face and sagely told him the story about the four blind wise men all trying to understand an elephant by touch. You remember that tale. One touched the trunk and thought it was snake-like, one touched the side and perceived it differently, and so forth. When I was done, Paul was as perplexed as ever but pretended to have learned something about reality by listening to another of Dad's stories.

To understand the nature of High Performance it is helpful to view it from several different vantage points as well. I'll start from a distance with a more macro view, and zero in as we go. Peter Senge, in his 1990 book *The Fifth Discipline*, introduced the business world to the concept of the Learning Organization. As is so often the case, he merely made popular the collective wisdom of the previous two decades. Forward-thinking, organizational leaders have long realized that continuous learning, what TQM (Total Quality Management) called "continuous improvement," has always been necessary for progress. Others have discussed the same topic but with less rigor. Ikujiro Nonaka, for example, described the phenomena as "knowledge-creating companies." But with the circulation of Senge's book, the concept took flight for the first time. Indeed, the book is as worth reading today, as it was when it was first published. A few of his examples may be dated, but the principles are still valid.

My take is a little different from his, but we are allied philosophically. The Cliff's Notes Version would take us on a path among five interrelated disciplines, each one an area for personal and organizational study and practice. I see the 30,000-foot view of High Performance as having a philosophical base comprised of the following. These are the presuppositions behind High Performance which individuals and companies need to investigate, study, and develop.

    I. Self Awareness
    II. Philosophical Platforms
    III. Shared Learnings
    IV. Making the Future Visible
    V. Aligned Thinking

I. Self-Awareness
Self Awareness sounds a lot like the cant of the 1960's or a clone of Maslow's hierarchy of needs. Most of us assume it will just happen if we go about our business. Sadly, most of

us do not spend a lot of time in self assessment until we get fired, the marriage coughs up a hairball, the step daughter walks out of the house, the son calls to tell us never to write again, or we have to face a medical crisis in our own or a loved one's life. We're so busy trying to become successful we lose our children or marriages in the process. Somehow we have erroneously learned to associate "self assessment" with "self absorption," and our churches and synagogues as well as our social critics and ancient mythologies warn us against such Narcissism. Besides, we, as business leaders, are often too busy to waste time "gazing at our navels."

On the other hand, high performers spend time learning about themselves and doing a systematic assessment of their personal, intellectual and emotional capital. Our businesses today demand more and more from us than ever in the past, and only those who know themselves inside and out, their strengths and their potential liabilities, will survive the very intense winnowing process of the third millennium. Not everyone is general manager material. Not everyone is comfortable with rapidly changing technologies. Not everyone is good with people. Not everyone values the strengths gained from working as a team. But everyone can grow by investing time and energy to understand what makes himself or herself tick.

Are you at your best in a staff function or a leadership role? Would you rather be out in sales or marketing dealing with people every day or in a lab titrating your favorite chemicals or playing with a Petri dish? If you are going to run an organization, are you more comfortable with a stable commodity business, a specialties business zipping out six new products a year, or walking in to a mess that has to be "turned around?" Morgan McCall sets out some handy guidelines in *The Lessons of Experience* on how to make the most of career opportunities to help managers sort out this part of self-mastery. Smart organizations will invest some time in their middle managers to help them figure out where their natural strengths lie.

Ed Schein's research in *Career Anchors* is also a valuable approach to help us understand where our real interests and talents lie. Are our competences in the technical and functional area of business, or do we want more autonomy and independence. Does aspiring to general managership excite us, or does providing a service or dedicating ourselves to a cause motivate us? Do we prefer the relative stability and security of being part of a big company or system, or are we more entrepreneurial in spirit. One size does not fit all. Part of our development of personal self-mastery is determining our best fit into our profession.

Many leaders these days employ a personal coach to assist them in moving toward personal high performance. They have spawned a whole new industry for executive coaches. Since we do a lot of manager coaching, we certainly appreciate that spawning. Business leaders have learned just what good athletes have learned over the years, that it is necessary to have a trusted personal coach with whom they can talk, confess, share, complain, bounce off ideas, and learn. It is the insightful leader who recognizes that those around her or him are usually too close to a business or a decision to provide objective counsel. In some senior leadership meetings, when an EVP dares to confront the pet project of the president, the silence is deafening. So, senior leaders often find themselves adrift wondering how they can continue to grow themselves while they encourage such growth in others.

Many senior leaders these days are rather lonely people. Who, after all, can they talk to? They know that most people working for them won't tell them the truth. The emperor may not have a stitch on, but no one, concerned about her or his own career, is about to say so. Most individuals tend to avoid pain and seek pleasure. Only moths fly into the flame willingly. Often the task of leadership is less about determining what is false or true but understanding what you cannot be told. Plausible deniability takes on many forms. The senior coach can occasionally be a conduit between that which can and cannot be communicated by those within the organization.

Who can leaders talk to if they have misgivings about their ability to lead the company effectively? Who do they go to if speaking in front of a group petrifies them? Who can they talk to if they don't have a clue how to get the stock price back up to $ 40 / share where it was when they were selected to lead the company 18 months ago? Who do they go to if web technology irritates them, chemical processes confuse them, and SAP makes them drink heavily and chain smoke? At least the kings and queens of past years had their court fools. They were the only ones who would speak the truth, usually coating it in laughter to make it more palatable. *Mary Poppins* taught us a similar truth: "A spoonful of sugar makes the medicine go down." The sad fact is that McArthur and Patton and Napoleon and Lee were right years ago. Leadership at the top is a lonely place to be. Who would want to be in the shoes of President Bush as he tried to decide how to respond to the terrorist attack on the United States on September 11, 2001?

The executive coach has filled that void for the business leader in the last several years in increasing numbers. We can coax, cajole, shadow, advise, warn, suggest and point out things that can help the executive become more effective on the job. Just as the star athlete's coach can rarely play the game as well as the athletes themselves can, so the executive coach rarely has the ability, background, or the desire to lead a $4 billion manufacturing company, but she or he does have the knack of pointing out things that can enhance the leader's performance. All of us, even popular leaders, routinely say things and do things oblivious to the unintended consequences. The coach can point these things out whether or not they are popular, because this is what we are being paid to do. For us there are consequences for not being honest. We get fired, and that is the way it should be.

This use of coaches, while enjoyed by senior high performers in the past, is relatively new at lower levels in the company. You know yourself in the past if you heard that Johnson, over in sales, was being helped by an outside coach, you probably formed a poor opinion of Johnson.

He must be weak; he needs help. "Oh, I guess they are trying to save Johnson." There was a stigma attached to "needing" coaching. Today it is quite the opposite. It is often a perk, and some leaders almost gleefully introduce coaches at meetings to their peers and teams. General Electric, Motorola, Virgin Airlines, PNC, Charles Schwab Corp., Volvo (Brazil), American Science and Engineering, Coors Brewing Company, Express Dairies (UK), Bagir (UK), Harley Davidson, and other High Performers make regular use of coaches at multiple levels of the company's leadership. The right coach can help the emerging leader understand organizational politics and dynamics. The coach can help a leader change behaviors that interfere with success, potential, and promotion.

One of the best ways an organization can foster the value of coaching is to make it part of a formal program in which high potential candidates participate. When all aspiring general managers get assigned a coach to work with them to understand organizational politics, hone their leadership styles, develop a clearer strategic framework for managing their business's, or work on personal development, the organization begins to change its view of coaching. Managers begin to look forward to the assistance they receive and not dread it. The upshot is that the return on investment on the coaching increases dramatically. Richard Branson, Tiger Woods, Derek Jeter and Andre Agassi are great today not because they attend motivational seminars on days off but because they each have a trusted personal coach.

The tool we have found to be the most insightful in helping us coach is the Myers-Briggs Type Indicator®. The form has been around for decades, and most of the basic concepts have existed since Carl Jung gave us the initial language in the 1920's, but we are just beginning to learn, at the threshold to the third millennium, how to use the indicator effectively and ethically to help people, families, couples, teams, and larger organizations understand one another. For insights regarding the MBTI®, see my book *True To Type*, a leader's guide to personality diversity. When appropriately used, the results can assist individuals in beginning to value differences that previously they may have seen merely as irritants at best. Once a group can have impressed on them that differences are not only OK, but also valuable, it can begin to value and leverage the intellectual capital available to the organization.

II. Philosophical Platforms

Philosophical Platforms (philosophers refer to these as pre-suppositions) are the systems, the frames of reference, or the underlying paradigms we assume are implicit as we approach our lives. They are pictures in our minds, sets of possibilities, about how things are organized. This is the second discipline that those who aspire to organizational leadership need to understand and spend time studying and investigating. All of us unconsciously act on these philosophical platforms everyday.

Some of these platforms are as simple as our implicit belief, that when we wake up in the morning, sit up in bed, and swing our feet over the side of our mattress to the floor, that they will stay planted on the floor, and we will not float haphazardly up into space. We do not think to ourselves, each day, "I wonder if gravity is functioning today. I hope no one has turned it off, today." It just is! The concept and its consequences are part of our philosophical framework. It is a presupposition.

Despite the fact that most of us are wed philosophically to the above assumption, it is totally irrational at heart. The philosopher Bertrand Russell once described the irrationality of such an empiricist view by describing the chicken's dilemma. Let's say on day one, a chicken gets up and walks outside the coop, clucks around, eats some grain and goes back inside. On day two, the same chicken, let's call her Gladys, gets up, walks outside, clucks around, eats some grain and goes back inside. On day 765, Gladys gets up and walks outside the coop, just as she has for the first two years of her life, clucks around, eats some grain, and Mr. Perdue grabs her and wrings her neck. Gladys goes to KFC for supper. What is Gladys' problem? Russell would say her presupposition is flawed. She simply had too little data on which to act. A mere 765 days of consistent response to the same situation is inadequate data to justify acting on that presupposition. The next time you get out of bed, think about Gladys before you float off.

Sometimes we are forced to think about these philosophical platforms consciously when we associate with a religious assembly or study them in schools, but more often they lie unanalyzed as the foundation of how we act and live. Is our worldview theistic, agnostic, or atheistic? Those three options sum up the total range of possibilities. Do we believe we live in a coherent, knowable universe or think that we are mere bits of cosmic fluff bantered about by fickle, irrational physical laws? Is our science based on unified field forces that systematize the quanta, or are we at the whim of Chaos Theory? Is our worldview naturalistic, existential, or nihilistic? Is our philosophy Hegelian, Kantian, Aristotelian, or Platonic? Remember these strange words we studied in a philosophy course in our dim past?

Evaluating our personal presuppositions boils down to Tolstoy's comment that the most important question a person can pose is "what happens to me when I die?" Once I answer that question, I can decide how to live for the rest of my life. That "how" is the set of unspoken assumptions we call our world view. If you lack such philosophical baggage, you can call it a mental model, but it is much more.

Cultures have philosophical platforms as well. Thomas S. Kuhn's *Structure of Scientific Revolutions* summed up the paradigmatic shifts that had transformed culture and science by the middle of the 20th century. Once a paradigm has been articulated and accepted, all the forces of society come into play to ensure it is correct. The paradigm predetermines the outcome until the next paradigm uproots it. Philosophers know this as the Hegelian dialectic, where thesis plus antithesis yield to a new synthesis. What appears as the arbitrary replacement of one view of business with another is the systematic succession of a new paradigm over an older one.

Depending on the model we choose, we embed the answer in our equation.

Remember that obviously corrupt philosophical platform Americans had in November 2000? Adults actually assumed that if they went to the polls and cast their votes they could elect a president that evening. No one ever articulated that sentiment; it was just assumed. It was the basis of the thought structure upon which people acted. It had happened that way for the previous fifty years. Then the circumstances in Florida showed us the limitation of that mental model, and it took three Florida state court decisions, two federal court decisions, and one U. S. Supreme Court decision, not to mention dust pans full of punched out chads, hundreds of jokes by Jay Leno and David Letterman, and more TV news hours than the OJ trial to inform us that the person voted for by the majority of Americans was not the president three weeks later. A corrupt mental model to be sure! Or, actually, it was an overriding model called the Electoral College, which had to be ingrained mentally, which proved the deciding factor. One set of presuppositions won out over the other. Hegel and Gladys both would have been delighted!

In business, it is a little different. Businesses need continually to understand what philosophical platform or mental model they are using as they do business day by day. Does your business have a current valid business model? Do employees know what it is, and can they execute it?

What are my assumptions about the marketplace?
How do I view my customer?
Who is my customer?
What is my market segment?
What is our competitive advantage?
What is my strategy?
Are we fast or slow cycle?
How do we innovate?

In the majority of traditional companies with which we work, the employees are still working off an old philosophical platform. The senior leadership team may have decided to be innovative and seek new frontiers, but the employees who are expected to make these innovations have been left behind. There has been little training in change and no training in innovation. They have read about the changes in the company newsletter or the weekly e-mail, but they do not know their part in the overall scheme.

When the dotcoms began to reproduce like tribbles, they taught us all a valuable lesson in business models. The old business model suggested that we evaluate a stock and the company's worth based largely on the stock's P/E ratio. The company's high earnings would justify a high stock price. We measured success by having the highest P/E ratio in our industry segment. Then along came the dotcoms. They didn't even have a P/E ratio! At best they had a P/P ratio. Price to Earnings wasn't a concern for them; many never turned a dime profit. They were in the business of selling a **Price** to **Promise** ratio. The old philosophical platform treated stocks like bonds. The dotcoms' presuppositions treated stocks like options.

Not infrequently, the senior executives with whom I work still see the Internet as some kind of freaky sideshow; they will not be ready yet to embrace a mental model in transition. They are worried about security concerns, high costs of entry, or the likelihood that all e-commerce will turn specialty businesses into commodity auction houses. Most have never been in a chat room, few have ever personally ordered something on line, and many think virtual reality is relegated to the *Matrix* or other cyber-geek movies. Some of them with whom I work think that checking their e-mail once a week puts them in the vanguard. On the contrary, new employees entering the workplace today are as comfortable in the VR world as we were in Sesame Street. Most of your kids use the computer to talk to their friends more than you use it to grow your business.

Our company began its own foray into understanding some of the implications of e-commerce seven years ago when we were asked to help pick up the pieces from the

5th failed SAP project that contacted us within the same year. It was increasingly clear that SAP projects were going bottom up for a number of reasons, but one reason was a senior leadership reluctance to change old ways of thinking—to install a new set of presuppositions. They spent the money, hired the big consulting companies to act as implementers, dedicated 150 people for two to three years, but they kept the same presuppositions. They changed the hardware and the wiring but failed to change the organization,

I have not been an early adapter, myself, when it comes to Internet technology, as my associates will be happy to tell you, but we do have a learning organization where they have challenged me to change and grow and learn from them every day. I now find myself in a home in Zionsville, Indiana (I mean rural!) with six computers (2 Mac's and 4 pc's), two Palm Pilots, four cell phones, one GPS indicator, one portable satellite phone, six telephone landlines, and one DSL coming into my office. In the last three years, we have bought three cars and two homes on the Internet. In the case of one of the cars and both of the homes, I never saw them in person until I owned them and was making payments, although I did tour the homes by videotape and the Internet. One of my cars, a Mitsubishi 3000 GT, I test drove on a Java-based simulation on line from the hot tub overlooking Big Stick ski run on the front porch of my ski lodge in Deer Valley, Utah. And, I am behind the times!

I could not have dreamed of doing that even five years ago. I hired a technology coach, talked with my fourteen-year old son, and within a month could at least recognize the potential of business on line. How up to date are you with the technology available to your business today?

The philosophical platforms are changing all around us. Do any of you, besides me, always pick the wrong line at the supermarket? I survey the landscape. I see four lines; one has six people with carts, one has five people with very large carts, and one line has only four people waiting, but one of the persons has two carts loaded like they are heading up the Amazon for a year. I, savvy shopper that I am, wisely pick aisle four with just two people carrying baskets. What happens? "PRICE CHECK AISLE FOUR!" Some nincompoop has lost his credit card and the woman behind him has a check bounce. I stand in line for 20 minutes watching the other people with huge carts zipping through lines 1-3 like water through a garden hose. I know some people who put themselves through that nonsense four-five times per week.

What if you didn't have to stand in line, anymore? That's a new mental model that looked attractive during the dot-com explosion of 1997. How many of you shop for groceries on line? That's right, groceries. If you don't, why don't you? How much time does it take you to shop and to travel to and from the market each time. How much is your time worth? In the year 2000, eleven per cent of groceries in major North American cities were ordered on the Internet, through Kozmo.com, Streamline.com, Webvan.com, or some other goodies.com. Groceries are a high touch product that the old mental model said people wanted to touch, smell, and in the case of Charmin, squeeze. That appeared to be a corrupt presupposition from 1997-2000.

But something went wrong. First, Streamline.com went belly up, then the largest of all the services, Webvan.com, disappeared from the scene in June 2001. Despite the failures, on-line grocery shopping still consumed 7 % of the market.

The model seemed to make sense. Brick and mortar shelf space is costly and getting more so. The average Kroger Supermarket stocks 40,000 items in each of its several stores. They might be out of stock of any item in any of the stores you might visit. The average remaining Internet grocer stocks 100,000 items at one location. Theoretically, you could e-mail your list before leaving work and they could deliver it by suppertime for free—no delivery charge, despite sine wave gas prices. No wasted time, no wasted gas, no traffic jams, no whining kids, just more time for you with relatively the same cost. Roughly two hours added back to your life. And, if you lived in New Jersey, you wouldn't have to bag your own groceries.

But the model collapsed; something was wrong with the philosophical platform that served as a foundation for the model. Cost was OK, convenience was OK, and quality was OK. But the unasked question was "why do people go to the supermarket to shop?" It turned out that for a shocking number of people, grocery shopping is a stimulant—it is a social activity. The community side of shopping was missing. Singles under 30 were going to the store to scan for potential mating partners while fondling the broccoli, and those over 60 were headed to the same place to talk to someone—anyone. Many banks faced the same problem in the 1990's when they had to retrench from full automation to kiosks and coffee rooms to attract the over 60 crowd back to the bank. Faulty presuppositions generated a flawed business model. What presuppositions are foundational to your current business model? Are they fundamentally flawed, or are they futuristic and sound?

For some products and some age groups, the model works just fine. My wife buys almost all of the clothes for our kids on line, most of our airline tickets on line, alumni football tickets for Wisconsin, Pacer Tickets, Indianapolis Colts season tickets, theater tickets, NCAA Playoff tickets, books, replacement parts for appliances, even my Breitling watch for Christmas, without visiting a brick and mortar store. Austin does his high school research on line, and Paul, at the age of five, studies Spanish and French on line.

Today, and I mean today, because the data will change before this book gets to its publisher, over 68 million people are in the on-line consumer group despite the failure of hundreds of B-C's in 2000 and 2001. Compare that with just 1.3 million people in 1993. Worldwide web traffic doubles every 98 days, and web sales account for 10% of the world's economic product. Despite the Clinton Administration's efforts to destroy Bill Gates' empire, 42 % of Americans polled think Bill Gates has made their life better, 52 % of homes in North America have rearranged their homes to accommodate a computer, and 83 % of the population considers the computer the most important product of the century. It even beat the pill and the Big Mac. By 2003, global e-commerce will amount to three trillion dollars.

Just look at how our language has changed. Now, many of our preteen kids talk easily about ISDN's, portals, packet switching, backbones, virtual reality, intermediation, reintermediation, bittablility, content management, unbundling, consumerization, cannibalizations, domains, and "getting Amazoned." What's that? Just ask Pitney Bowes, Federal Express, or your local Little Professor Bookstore. And of course there is POTS—plain old telephone system, probably a museum artifact in 2010. Most of these words do not pass muster yet in the spell check on my Windows 2000 Professional.

Today's philosophical platform tells me no customer, supplier, or business partner is more than five tenths of a second away, and that may be too long in a world where, as the Silicon Valley executives who still have jobs tell us,

Speed is God and Time is the Devil.

When I need a business partner today, I can just as easily look in Bangalore, India, Monteverde, Costa Rica, or Leverkusen, Germany as in Virginia Beach, Virginia. My corporate headquarters can just as easily be in the cobblestone village of Zionsville, Indiana (where it presently is), on Lombardy Avenue in Green Bay, Wisconsin, on Asbury Avenue in Ocean City, New Jersey, or on Peachtree Street in Atlanta, Georgia. Geography is almost irrelevant. Today, e-literacy boils down to the matter of securing a completely new education on business and management.

If you are more than eight years into a career, it is more about forgetting what you know than it is about learning something new.

Today, we are just exploring the fringes of Internet possibilities for business, and the future is already being re-vectored toward a new model—the Grid. A new philosophical platform demands a new way of understanding available memory and where that memory has to be located geographically. The commercial payoff could be huge, and the impact it will have on production and R & D, will rock the foundations of the corporate world. Two thirds of our struggle will be in abandoning outdated belief systems and ditching presuppositions that no longer work.

It is a leadership task to challenge, on a routine basis, the existing philosophical platform to ensure the company is not being bypassed by the competition. Too often, the company's annual leadership conference is held just to bless the existing mental model and to hear the chairman's concerns about revenue and stock price. The leaders congregate to play some golf, hand out the annual chairman's awards, smoke cigars and play cards, while the mavericks and real star performers meet in the bars and hot tubs to argue about the lack of innovation and leadership in the company. I can think of at least five companies, right now, who will call me as soon as they buy this book, claiming I am talking about them in this example.

High Performing companies will use the same meeting to challenge all the models they currently use. They use the meeting to think differently and to challenge themselves to grow and learn and to embrace a different philosophical platform. If the senior leadership does not encourage employees routinely to challenge the existing business models and marketing presuppositions acted on by the company, they will lead it to mediocrity or the tar pits. The natural scientific revolution in our presuppositions for how businesses should function means persistently

changing how we change.

III. Ability to Learn and to Transfer Learnings
The third philosophical underpinning for High Performance is developing the ability to learn from one

another and to transfer the learnings. Productive work-places create a community of incessant learning. In other words, we need to be cognizant of what others are doing well. This might be other people in the company in a different business unit, or it might be a team in a different company or industry; it is the wise dog that trots about to find the bone. Smart companies systematically share learnings between divisions, stand-alone businesses, and business teams. They break down walls between parochial business silos and learn from one another. This is one discipline I find most companies do badly. One person doesn't offer suggestions because doing so is perceived as meddling, and another doesn't ask for help because doing so is perceived as a weakness. What silliness! We need to share ideas, understand what others are doing, and build community across the organization.

Worse, yet, is that sometimes we don't even know what the other division is doing. Maybe I have products I use in my Crop Protection Division that could have efficacy in the pharmaceutical division. Where and when do we share research data? How does a researcher in pharmaceuticals in Danbury, discover what Dr. Franks in the crop protection division is doing in Kansas City? Most large and complex organizations are so stove-piped and insular that very little real knowledge leaks out. It is similar to a California aircraft research facility where every time an experimental aircraft is moved, lights flash, doors are closed, and sirens sound warning all employees of a temporary lock down so the left hand does not know what the right one is doing. There, it may be necessary for security; in most other companies it happens out of benign neglect, parochialism or fear.

By the way, Lockheed Martin is one large company that is approaching the problem of sharing information correctly. They have an innovative program of integrated business and interpersonal development in partnership with Carnegie Mellon University's Graduate School of Industrial Administration, through which they put all managers. One of the highlights of the program is the encouragement participants get from senior leaders to challenge the existing philosophical platforms the company espouses and to share learnings across business units and geographical regions. The company's leadership has begun to change the culture from one in relative financial disarray in 1999 to one preparing the company for great success in the third millennium. The F-35 Joint Strike Fighter will be in sound production hands when Lockheed Martin is awarded the "winner take all" contract.

The existing systems of reward and recognition, budgeting and annual appraisals often encourage business units or divisions to compete against each other. Sales groups often set up competition, matching the results of one group against the other, in the mistaken belief that such competition will increase sales or enhance performance. Such groups rarely share information because sharing information might give the edge to the other team.

Often the closest we get to sharing ideas systematically is to investigate the best practices in our industry or peer group. The company hires one of the big five consulting companies for a couple hundred thousand dollars to investigate the best practices in the industry—find out what the competition is doing well. They go to their computer database and print off thirty-six pages of best practices in the industry or among your peer group (probably the same report they sent to six other clients this year) and send them to you with a large invoice personalized just for you. You get to learn the best practices out there and decide which ones you want to implement over the next year. All that process guarantees is that when the competition goes belly up, you will be right there next to them taking their pulse. Where is the competitive advantage in that process?

If you are going to invest in some best practice analysis, it ought to be "future best practices." I remember watching the recent NBA playoffs, and during one game being played by the Toronto Raptors, the TV cameras zoomed in on Canadian national hero and basketball super fan,

Wayne Gretzy, sitting in the front row. Many years ago when asked what made him so great, Gretzy replied, "I am great because I never skate to where the puck is." When the reporter queried him as to what he meant, Gretzy replied, "I skate to where the puck is going to be." That is future best practices. They are the only ones worth investigating.

Many years ago when I was an Associate Professor on the academic faculty of West Point, I was the coach and faculty advisor to the West Point Cadet Handball Team. Year in and year out we would get highly motivated, super fit young athletes, bursting with testosterone. They would race around the court with incredible energy and often demolished the competition with their sheer physical fitness. Once each year, just as a small lesson in humility, I would take the cadets to the New York City YMCA or to the DAC (Downtown Athletic Club) for a day of competition. These places are where old jocks like me hang out to play sports. Two 19-year old cadets would be waiting in the handball court for their competition, probably bouncing on their toes and high fiving while they waited impatiently. Then, in they would come; both over 55, both overweight, one bald, one with an earring, both with bad knees in leather braces, one whose chest had been cracked twice, one with a noticeable limp, and both smelling of Ben Gay. The cadets would look up at me in the balcony with a quizzical look wondering why I had bothered to waste their time.

After the cadets had lost 21-5, 21-3, 21-11, we would discuss their strategy and try to understand why they had been beaten so badly by such an "inferior foe." The cadets would fly around the court following the ball with lightening speed and sometimes get there before the ball—best practices, if you will. The "crusty old guys," the super savvy competition, would hit the ball and casually walk or limp to where it would be after its third or fourth bounce and put it away for a kill shot—future best practices. As we examine future best practices, we prepare the organization for exciting learnings.

**What is the most powerful learning your team
or your organization has had at work, and what
conditions made it possible? If you can't think of
one, the company is in trouble.**

Of course we can't invest time in team learnings until we
learn what a team is and until we understand the philosophical platform on which the business routinely acts. We
can't do any of that until we understand our personal belief
systems, and we can't do that until we spend some time
exploring personal self-mastery. There is no short cut to
high performance. Now we are ready for the hard work.

IV. Vision Alignment

The fourth block in the philosophical foundation for High
Performance pertains to the "V" word. It is often talked
about, sometimes believed, and routinely hung on conference room walls and typed on wallet-sized cards to be
issued to the customer along with the Quality Policy. It is
usually developed badly, understood poorly, executed errat-
ically, and rarely tied to the business. The reason most
visions fail to compel interest or drive the business is that
the wrong people develop it, and little effort is given to
aligning the organization with it. Having a **Shared Vision**
is a prerequisite for generating High Performance.

Too often the scenario looks like this. The management
team goes off for a team building session with a consultant
at the local Marriott Hotel. They golf for one afternoon
and work for a day and a half. Two days later they return
with a three-paragraph vision statement for the organization. The vision looks remarkably similar to the previous
twenty vision statements that the same consultants helped
organizations to develop. Whose vision is it? It's the leadership team's and no one else's. That team, then, needs to
spend the next two years trying to sell their vision to the
organization. Meanwhile, nothing changes. It is no wonder
then that many business leaders see vision statements as
complete wastes of time and money. Their experience in
the past has been less than helpful.

Go with me to your house. Enter by the front door and make your way down to the kitchen. Walk up to your side-by-side refrigerator and open the door. Go to that plastic crisper drawer down at the bottom and pull the drawer open. Reach in and take out the large, fresh lemon you purchased yesterday. Take the lemon over to your DuPont Corion counter top. Take out the sharpest knife you have and cut the lemon in half. Now, take the largest half of the lemon and put it up to your mouth and suck on the lemon; chew on the side of the lemon and let the juice drip into your mouth.

Is anything happening in your mouth? Why does it happen? Forget Pavlov; it happens because the brain is the dumbest organ in the body!

The brain does not know the difference between a real lemon and the thought of one. It sends the same signal to the body!

The brain compels; it says act, do, perform, produce! Think about the power of that knowledge. What that means is that if you can create a vision of success for your team, for your organization, for your company, you CAN NOT FAIL. I defy you to try! The brain will demand performance. That is powerful knowledge. There is nothing touchy-feely about a vision done right. It is a compelling business principle to which you can tie your strategy.

Once we have the vision our work is not done. Remember, the key is having a "shared" vision. That compels the organization's leadership to strive constantly to create alignment between why each employee shows up to work each day and the organization's vision. Henry Ford is noted as saying, "why is it, that every time when I have a job to fill, and all I need is another pair of hands, I get a whole person every time." It's a bummer. We have all these "whole persons" with different needs, expectations, talents, and motivations, and somehow the leaders throughout the organization have to motivate all of them toward the same goal. That process is called "alignment."

Do you have employees who feel they don't fit in or don't belong? What are you going to do about it? The lack of alignment translates into mediocre performance. Ethics in business may be little more than asking, "how should I behave, once I know I belong?" In many individuals, the need to belong is fundamental. Too often, we relegate this one to the arena of Human Resources. That is a mistake. Organizational alignment is a senior leadership responsibility.

V. Aligned Thinking

Once we have spent time understanding the first four fundamental underpinnings of High Performance, we can begin to see the whole picture. But, after we have consciously increased our self-knowledge, investigated and challenged our existing frames of reference, shared learnings broadly across the company, developed a shared vision, and begun to create alignment between the company's vision and why each employee comes to work each day, we can begin to think systemically. Until then, not a prayer! I call this one Aligned Thinking. It is a variety of orthomolecular organizational development (OOD). Rather than treat the symptoms as so many doctors do these days, or treat the specific infection, orthomolecular doctors treat the patient at the cellular level; orthomolecular physicians treat the patient holistically or systemically. They seek to understand how all the body's systems (gastro-intestinal, cardio-vascular, pulmonary, and others) work together for good health and high physical performance. The High Performance Organization needs to embrace a similar philosophy.

In the past, we tended to treat organizational problems from a more isolated perspective. If we tried to fix the big three—People, Finances, and Technology—we did it one at a time. If people were the problem we hired more, and then the mental model changed and for the past ten years we fired more. Sometimes, it seems we fired more than we ever hired (see the chapter entitled "The Corporate Nip and Tuck" in my book, entitled *Taming The Scorpion: Preparing Business for the Third Millennium*). Of course, when we fire people we then need to buy more technology to make up for the people fired. But new technology demands expenditure of more money. If we needed new technology, SAP for example, that cost more money—usually three times what the implementing big 5 consulting company predicted—and, once implemented, cost many more people their jobs. If we have to cut costs, than we have to take heads or... Eventually we "got it." We figured out that any time we touched one of the three, changes impacted the other two. We had to learn to think systemically. Aligned Thinking tends to see the organization as a fragile mobile. A change in any one of the three, causes changes in the others. It is the ability to see the whole and the parts and how they all interact to produce the results we are getting.

Systemic thinking must become an enterprise-wide expectation. People at all levels must be engaged to think continually about the interdependence of finances, people, and technology. Employees have to be held accountable for always asking, "how do my actions impact the other departments, teams. SBU's, or divisions?" Continuous Aligned Thinking builds an organization of collaborative learning.

Every organization is perfectly designed to get the results it gets. If you don't like your results, change your organization.

From thirty thousand feet, the journey to High Performance looks rather simple. Five philosophical underpinnings consciously acted on lead us there irrevocably. Let's drop down to the ten thousand foot view. Here the terrain looks a little rockier. The path is less clear. The changes required seem a bit more perplexing. The dangers are much less theoretical. The chance for failure is greater. Is your organization ready to begin the journey?

CHAPTER SIX

Ready, Get Set, Go

Before we look at the characteristics of high performing corporations, we ought to try to figure out if the organization is ready. We routinely administer a survey such as the one that follows to key players to try to ascertain the current tenor—where the organization stands. How would your team score on the following? How would your employees answer the following questions?

Circle the number that reflects your view of each question. When you finish all twenty questions, sum the numerical responses. Hint: be brutally honest.

High Performance Readiness Checklist

1. Are individuals' suggestions for change valued and solicited or regarded as, at best, necessary inconveniences?

1   2   3   4   5   6   7   8   9   10
inconveniences   *valued and solicited*

2. Do team members share their concerns, fears, and passions with peers?

1   2   3   4   5   6   7   8   9   10
never   *frequently*

3. When debate or conflict occurs, are settlements accomplished fairly or are "favorites" trusted and supported?

1   2   3   4   5   6   7   8   9   10
"favorites" are trusted   *settlements are mediated fairly*

4. Is management seen as independent and "empowered" or a pawn of senior leadership?

1   2   3   4   5   6   7   8   9   10

a pawn   *independent and empowered*

5. Do your employees have a clear vision of the business's future?

1   2   3   4   5   6   7   8   9   10

no   *we have a clear published vision*

6. Would employees say they have "buy-in" to the company's vision?

1   2   3   4   5   6   7   8   9   10

no, many employees do not know it   *we participated in the process and "buy in"*

7. Do leaders in your organization share credit for success with others?

1   2   3   4   5   6   7   8   9   10

no   *yes, frequently*

8. Do team members "go to bat" for one another if someone is unfairly criticized?

1   2   3   4   5   6   7   8   9   10

no   *yes, frequently*

9. Does your group / team act on a consistent set of agreed upon values?

1   2   3   4   5   6   7   8   9   10

no, it is ad hoc   *yes*

10. Would your employees say they value the contributions made by your management team?

1   2   3   4   5   6   7   8   9   10

no   *yes, our impact is clear*

11. Do employees trust senior management to lead them through significant changes?

1   2   3   4   5   6   7   8   9   10

no, there is a lack of credibility   *yes, they depend on senior management*

12. Is there an open flow of communication between employees, their immediate supervisors, and senior management?

1	2	3	4	5	6	7	8	9	10

no, there is fear   *communication is valued*

13. Do middle managers believe they are valued as company resources?

1	2	3	4	5	6	7	8	9	10

no, they are left out   *they are indispensable*

14. Does your management team understand your company's core competencies and align its businesses and strategies accordingly?

1	2	3	4	5	6	7	8	9	10

no   *this is an ongoing priority*

15. Are you a learning organization or a learning disabled (reactive) organization?

1	2	3	4	5	6	7	8	9	10

disabled and reactive   *constantly learning and acting*

16. Is there a clear path of career progression for your employees?

1	2	3	4	5	6	7	8	9	10

not for most individuals   *all know requirements*
for getting from a-z

17. Are team members held accountable for acting and deciding on the basis of agreed upon values?

1	2	3	4	5	6	7	8	9	10

no, we have no norms   *yes, we have clear*
operating principles

18. Is there a clear set of metrics you monitor to see how well your team is doing to achieve its vision?

1	2	3	4	5	6	7	8	9	10

no, not beyond finance and   *we chart our progress*
safety   *vigorously and openly*

19. Are our management team meetings timely and productive?

1   2   3   4   5   6   7   8   9   10
they are ineffective   highly productive and supportive

20. If you invited 3-4 employees to sit in on your management team meetings on a rotating basis, just to listen and learn, would they be impressed by your ability to run the company or discouraged and fearful?

1   2   3   4   5   6   7   8   9   10
they would seek other   our reputation as leaders
employment immediately   would be enhanced

High performance organizations score routinely over 140 on the above survey. If your organizational average is less than 100, you have some work to do in moving toward the criteria below.

CHAPTER SEVEN

Ten Thousand Foot High Performance

Once every year or so, we gather our core consultants and the senior leaders from some of our major clients, and we invite them to a conference on a topic of mutual interest. In the past several years we have gathered at our company's executive retreat in Deer Valley, Utah, the site of the 2002 Winter Olympics. We call these meetings Conversations in Deer Valley. There, amid the beauty of the snow-covered Wasatch Mountains, we talk and we argue and we strive for clarity about issues that can revolutionize how companies do businesses.

At our last conference, the topic was Business High Performance. What is it? What are its elements? How do we achieve it? How do we recognize it? How do we know when we are there? The business leaders at the last meeting, representing a broad spectrum of industries, identified eleven traits that in their opinion characterized High Performance.

In the year since, we have presented these traits in the business schools of Stanford University, Carnegie Mellon University, Wharton, The University of Virginia, University of Southern California, The University of Georgia, MIT, Columbia, Duke University, The University of Pittsburgh, Old Dominion University, The University of Michigan, Ball State, and Georgia Tech. We have also discussed them with the leadership of multi-national corporations in China, Belgium, Germany, Japan, Romania, France, Canada, Mexico, Singapore, Brazil, India, Nigeria, Great Britain, Australia, Vietnam, Russia, and The United States. Their feed back in each case roughly translates to the following traits being the most important indices to which they pay attention.

Trait 1: Actively Create a Learning Organization.
We all have heard about them. I assume we all want to work in one. We just don't know what one is or how to form one. The alternative, clearly, is not attractive.

At its heart, **a learning organization is one that is skilled at acquiring, sharing, and generating, as rapidly as possible, new learnings and in changing systems, procedures, and behaviors to reflect the new learnings.** What most senior leaders bemoan are those individuals in their organizations who are so tied to the past that they refuse to adopt new technologies or ways of thinking. Shelf after shelf of policy and procedure manuals exist as officially sanctioned ways of saying no to changes rather than enabling performance. Unfortunately, the certainties of the past become the problems of the present.

Recently, we were hired to run an e-business conference for a large, multi-national, Fortune 100 Company. About 200 senior leaders from around the world had been brought together to hear about some of the e-commerce initiatives recently begun in the company. Our assigned task was to package the conference and to challenge the company's leadership to go beyond their current thinking about simply "buying and selling stuff on line"; that's all e-commerce really is. We wanted to stretch them into seeing more strategic e-business opportunities. I led the session off with the keynote address and was then followed by four other creative speakers from among our senior consultants, each of whom stretched the audience in new ways.

By the time Ira, our creative Internet guru who has built our virtual corporation from scratch, finished his presentation on holding virtual meetings in virtual conference rooms, a presentation laced with VR this and VR that, and had demonstrated the capability with two of our ESI team members who were, at the time, working in different countries, the faces of the senior executives in the room had changed character and the room had a palpable feeling of tension.

Ira had just demonstrated a system using real time video and voice over I T which put community and human intercourse back into a sterile Internet world of distant communication—and it worked. Theirs, on the other hand, did not. Because of insufficient training and apparently spotty IS support, managers were constantly frustrated by e-mail and expensive teleconferencing systems that caused continuous problems. The question was, who would speak up? Who would be bold enough to point out the shortcomings of a dominant Information Systems (IS) Department? In this case it fell to the chairman to rise to his feet and take on Ira and Bill Gates collectively by pointing out the problems of the overly-complex systems that the IS department had implemented. He didn't blame any one or any group; he simply admitted the frustrations he personally had with using the existing technologies. Many people in the room had been having problems with the system, but no one wanted to look incompetent or, worse yet, at an e-commerce meeting, not current with the prevailing technology.

The room was silent. The looks on the faces of the other 200 senior people told the tale. The chairman had just expressed the very frustration so many of them were feeling. The whole group knew the company was going NO WHERE with e-business as long as many of the senior leaders in the corporation were disenfranchised from the new technology. The honesty he had expressed underscores much of the disconnect today between the promise and potential of the Internet, and the paranoia surrounding its use. The technology is becoming available far quicker than our means to embrace it and make sense out of it. Our information systems revolution is a dual bargain. Those who have to use it must be open-minded and willing to embrace the new technology and ideas. On the other hand, the IS people cannot afford the arrogance of technological wizards who can design a system only for other techno-wizards.

We certainly wouldn't respect parents who tried to motivate children to learn but who, themselves, did not respect learning and, indeed, repudiated new learnings. Their personal behavior reflects their true intellectual posture. The business world is no different. Leaders must set the pattern for those whom they supervise. If foremen, supervisors, and middle managers have stopped learning—the business equivalent of book burning—they will inspire little growth or innovation in those they supervise. It doesn't take the appointment of a pricey CLO (Chief Learning Officer) to cultivate a learning organization. It takes an organization and organizational leaders who constantly attune themselves with the marketplace and the environment around it. It adapts and learns. All of us must be continuous learners and teachers.

Let's be honest. Almost every part of your business these days is a commodity. The hamburger is still just a hamburger at Burger King, Hardees, MacDonalds, or White Tower, regardless of whether it is round or square, boiled, fried, grilled, or barbecued. If you sell training modules, I can go to forty other websites these days and look at training modules offered on-line, live, via video tape, cassette tape, capable of being downloaded, or printed out in pamphlets. I can go to any of the dozen magazines I get each month and order materials by Pfeiffer, HRDQ, CAPT, HD Press, Harvard University Press, and others. They are all the same! They just have different labels, titles, and prices. If I sell chemical products, I can just as easily contact CheMatch.com, Plasticsnet.com, Powerfarm.com, or ChemConnect.com as contact you. In fact, I'll probably get a better price. In a conversation I had with a senior vice president in Lockheed Martin Space Systems last week, he mentioned that he received mailings for a dozen different kinds of team training each month from different vendors.

Often it was impossible to differentiate between them. Everything has become a potential commodity.

Today, the only true competitive advantage is your ability to learn and to learn faster than the competition.

Watch a new team come together in your organization, and take note of the behaviors it manifests. How fast does it learn or embrace new behaviors?

1. How is leadership established? How does everyone know who is in charge?
2. What leader behaviors are demonstrated? Would you do it the same way?
3. How are roles and responsibilities established?
4. What are the competencies required for each task? How are they identified and communicated? How are individuals held accountable for performance?
5. How are group decisions made?
6. Are there areas of conflict? Are they always the same? Are the same individuals involved?
7. How is conflict within the group handled?
8. Is there evidence of the group's learning from the conflict?
9. What values do you observe being acted upon?
10. How involved are all of the team members? Are there outliers? How does the group bring the outliers back in?
11. How does the group handle failure?
12. How does the group handle success?
13. How does the group identify where certain expertise resides?
14. Are individuals held accountable for their performance?
15. What methods does the group employ to keep constant learnings in front of the entire group?

Trait 2: Engender a Business Sense at Every Level of the Organization.
How does your company do this? If you were asked how you teach your employees "business" and how to think and

act like a "business" person, what would your response be? Do you do anything at all? The failure to engender a business sense in employees is the single biggest failure on the part of most businesses, today. We train in skills; we train in safety; we sometimes train in diversity, teams, and developmental issues; sometimes, we even give classes in benefits or other human resources issues. But most companies would not even know where to begin to develop a business sense.

We expect certain people to come to the company with formal credentials, MBA degrees, or other business related degrees. These people we call "business leaders" and give them groups and divisions to manage. But the employees, who have to make decisions day by day on quality, safety, manufacturing excellence, production, do so day by day often without understanding the implications on the "business." Why should we expect them to be enthusiastic about their jobs when they don't know what their job contributes to the overall success of the company?

Having a "business sense," good old business common sense, is a cognitive skill that can be developed. It's not that some have the ability and others don't. The point is that some people have had the opportunity to develop it and others have not. Some have elected to take that opportunity, and some have not. We are constantly defined by our choices. These skills can be as basic as teaching a shift of Teamsters on a color concentrates team in Coventry, Rhode Island the basics of finances and how to read a profit and loss statement, so they can take ownership of overtime pay to skills as complex as aligning business strategies with core competencies and assessing the company's overall competitive advantage. When people at every level of the organization understand the basics of the business, they are freed up to make a myriad of decisions that previously were kicked upstairs at least two levels too far. Creating a business sense realigns the decision making process, creates ownership at every level of the business, and generates innovativeness up and down the organization.

How well do your managers and supervisors understand the nature of the business they are charged with running? If you want to develop the level of understanding regarding your company's business strategy and core competencies, ask around, facilitate a search conference, hold some meetings to discuss some of the following:

1. What is your company's strategic intent?
2. Is your main intent obtaining margin or gaining market share?
3. Do you intend to be a market leader or a close follower?
4. Is your business global or international in scope?
5. What are your company's core competencies?
6. Where do you excel: low costs, economies of scale, R&D, manufacturing excellence, managing brand equity, or what?
7. What are the current or required strategic alliances (both internal and external) that enable your business to succeed?
8. What are the perceived shortcomings of the business?

These are vital questions. What would the level of sophistication be in the responses you receive from people in your company? Is this a foreign language to you? Would it be to them? Would they think you had lost it or just came back from graduate school if you started talking this way?

If your leaders were asked to assess the company's overall competitive advantage, how would they do discussing the following?

1. From a client's perspective, what differentiates your company?
2. Why should I buy from you?
3. Are sales transactional or consultative?
4. How does your model, Business-Business, Business-Consumer, or Consumer-Consumer impact your strategy?
5. How sustainable is your competitive advantage in terms of months or years? Is it renewable? What

would it take to renew it?

6. What are the environmental constraints that impact your advantage: are they budgets, technologies, intellectual capital, or market readiness?
7. Are there any forces outside your traditional industry that may threaten your competitive posture?
8. In short, what keeps your leaders up at night?
9. What keeps you up at night?

How well does the company's culture serve as an infrastructure to support the business strategy? What characteristics define the culture? What are the dynamics between strategic business units? Are they insulated and independent, or is there some creative synergy in the white space that makes 2+2 more than 5. How well is knowledge transferred and applied between, within, and across business units?

Understanding all of this may seem like a tall order, but as I constantly ask the youth soccer team I coach, "How good do you want to be?" As a business, how important is it to you to achieve High Performance? Here is a simple litmus test. Pick 5 of your employees from different levels of the company's hierarchy and pose two simple questions.

1. What is your company's competitive posture within the industry?
2. What is your view on the company's value creation process five years from now?

The blank stares you will generate by these simple questions should send shivers down your spine. These are not topics we study in a college class and then forget. We don't brainstorm these issues once every five years and collect the answers on flip charts to be typed up by the training department. These questions are ones that are posed by every employee, every day, in every functional area of High Performing businesses.

Employees in high performing companies talk about these

issues over coffee, at the water fountain, at lunch, in the smoke shack, and at team and staff meetings on a routine basis. They are comfortable talking about:

1. Reading and interpreting P&L's
2. Pro's and con's of in-house vs. out-house R&D
3. Putting together a business plan
4. Knowing where their pet projects are in the innovation pipeline
5. Coaching vs. managing vs. leading—what do they do best? Where do they need help?
6. Understanding the differences between commodity and specialty businesses
7. Working through the elements of an organizational analysis
8. Negotiating with contesting parties
9. Managing consultants
10. Pricing do's and don't's
11. Working with union employees
12. Using different decision-making methodologies
13. Interviewing potentially new employees skillfully
14. Implementing quality processes and measures
15. Implementing and using SAP or equivalent enterprise-wide systems
16. Meeting management skills
17. Understanding the pro's and con's of benchmarking
18. Building a business library
19. Shaping change in the organization
20. Creating a compelling story that can engage people at every level of your company, and
21. Mentoring.

How well does your company stack up in having a business sense? If you are relying on the B-schools to develop it, you will never be able to spend enough money to get the job done. The task is a leadership responsibility. Sometimes this task requires formal mentoring, sometimes classes on specific topics, sometimes the hiring of outside consultants who specialize in developing organizational leaders. Sometimes it comes from a business culture that encourages all leaders to travel with junior mentees to

meetings, negotiations, and high-level staff meetings, just to let the juniors be back- benchers and listen to the kinds of discussions that take place among senior leaders as they try to guide the business. This simple approach to growing future business leaders is mentoring at its best.
Organizations like General Electric, Monsanto, Hoechst, Marriott International, and Corpus Christi Research Center (during the old Celanese days) are superb at raising up junior leaders with real business savvy. Some corporations like Great Lakes Chemical, Ameritech, GRS, Samsung, GAF, and Ensaldo can drive high performing people away.

Trait 3: Plan for Systematic Obsolescence.
Who is in charge of systematic renewal for your company? Who should be in charge? Too often the nuts and bolts of this aspect of High Performance are pawned off to R&D or to the New Business Development folks. Part of every business meeting should include time for systematic renewal. The full time task of your competition is to take market share from you, obsolete your best products, and to beat you to the punch. That knowledge requires that your primary task is to plan for your own systematic obsolescence by trying to replace your most important product. It is critical that you do it before your competition does.

Microsoft is superb at doing this. Every product that hits the shelves, whether it is Windows 98, Windows 2000, or Windows XP has its demise built into it, by what it includes and what it does not include. The replacement product is planned and begun before the soon to be replaced product is sold. Michael Porter's S curve for understanding business development from Phase I to Phase III demands a periodic reintegration of the curve to keep late Phase II organizations from dying off in Phase III. One way of integrating that curve is by jumpstarting your own products. When Underwood told us back in the 1980's how proud they were to have 85% of the typewriter market, the death knell was sounding. Some companies are content to ride their sacred cows into the tar pits.

On the other hand, consider the gutsy move when large, successful Hoechst, A. G. shifted its entire energies in the 1990's from chemicals and fibers to pharmaceuticals and decided to build its future as largely a holding company in the life sciences field. People in the chemical industry thought Jürgen Dormann, CEO of Hoechst, A.G. was crazy, and he got very low marks from the American side of Hoechst Celanese, who, as a result of the changes, ceased to exist in 1998 after a decade and a half of spotty performance. Several years after the Hoechst move, a senior Bayer business leader in Leverkusen, Germany told me, "we are watching the Hoechst experiment very carefully, praying that they fail." The implication was that if Hoechst was right in their massive corporate restructuring and paradigm shift, Bayer would have to follow suit. Today the chemical industry is imploding within. Hoechst anticipated the implosion.

Trait 4: Demand Customer Focus Throughout the Corporation.

I remember hearing Vince Calarco, Chairman and CEO of Crompton Corporation, one time wryly challenging his senior leaders to become more customer focused by saying he had "tried for years to figure out how to run a business without customers," and hadn't figured out a way yet. Despite his tongue in cheek, many of you could probably name a company you had to work with in the last month that treated you, as the customer, as an inconvenience. No fair, now, naming an airline. They are too easy to mock. I guess it would be nice if we could get away with it, but those pesky customers are always demanding more and more for less and less. Too often, companies relegate the need to meet customer expectations to the customer service function or a small group of people wearing headsets as they answer customer complaints and try to get production planners to deliver on the outlandish promises made by hungry sales persons.

Customer service in high performing companies becomes a full-time job for every employee. We like to have our clients participate in action learning labs—creative business simulations involving live customers—that catch employees in the act of being themselves. Time and again, participants can see demonstratively the differences in performance and productivity that occur when every employee, every minute has as her or his chief consideration, "how is what I am doing right now directly impacting the customer?"

I will readily admit that I have become the customer from hell. Haven't you? As money is in shorter supply, and the prices we pay for appliances, automobiles, meals in restaurants, rental cars, hotel rooms, and my favorite—airline seats—go higher and higher, I certainly demand more and more. During the years 2000 and 2001 airlines complained about the rise in cases of air rage, despite the fact that they couldn't keep track of our luggage, destroyed it when it did arrive on time, cancelled more and more flights because they were under subscribed, arrived late more often, and gave us less and less service. It surprises me that there were not more cases of air rage. The violence is never warranted, but the rage, often more than warranted as we are kept in the dark, told nothing, sometimes de-iced three times in Newark before we can take off for Boston, kept sitting in a stuffy steel casket full of crying children for hours in O' Hare because American Eagle decides to go on strike during the holiday rush, or face slowdown after slowdown by United as they inconvenience us, the customers who pay their salaries, because they don't think they earn enough for the inconveniences they generate.

Since the tragic events of 911 and the federal bailout of the airlines, service has gotten predictably worse. Food service has been cut, carry on baggage has become more limited, and flights, which are now more inconvenient than ever, are more expensive. The airlines pretend all the measures they are taking provide better security. Those of us who are frequent fliers know that little has changed since 911, except that we now get less for more. Even those airlines which were in serious financial trouble before 911 and would have been mercifully eliminated through normal market forces got bailed out with American tax money. I fear we will continue to expect less from the airlines while they charge us more and try to justify all their actions on non- existent security improvements.

Well, whatever your business, meet your new business partner. In the future, I, as your customer, will demand to be more and more involved in your business. Your major customers increasingly will expect to participate in your quality process, to assist you in your R&D, and be included in major decisions made. Expect to be more involved with business partners at every level of performance. Even among competitors, companies will share more and more information, even formerly proprietary data, to meet customer expectations.

Trait 5: Communicate a Value Proposition that Differentiates you from the Competition.

When I work with individual entrepreneurs or company teams to build a business plan in support of their idea or product, one question I always ask is "what is your unique factor?" It is the business equivalent of asking a person, "who do you think you are?" "Why should I bother listening to you?" As a venture capitalist or a dotcom angel, I have an absolute right to ask, "Why should I bother listening to you?" Since I am funding the show, I will demand to know the unique factor that will compel people to buy your technology, service, or product.

Consider the way Wal-Mart Stores, Inc. changed the model for how department store chains did business? If Taco Bell, Wendy's, or Hardees decides to open a new store, they pick the busiest corners on the busiest streets, in the busiest parts of town. In fact, most of them pop up in exactly the same place. Not unusually, there are three to four fast food restaurants within the same block. Sam Walton changed the model. He constructed his stores in Toad Suck, Arkansas, Ridgecrest, California, and Lick Skillet, Indiana. He broke the rules. Wal-Mart's employees' value proposition is that they are real people, talking like real people when you walk in the door. They treat the customer like real people, and they go wherever real people need their products.

If you want to be pampered while you shop for high-end brand name products, you have come to the wrong store. If you want to go shopping in dirty jeans and cut-off t-shirts and have somebody say "Hi!" to you as you walk into the front door, go visit Sam's, but leave your Guccis at home tucked under your Select Comfort Bed.

Hummer's value proposition is a little different. They promise to sell you one ugly vehicle that will drive like a truck, smell like a truck, handle like a truck, and may not fit into your garage. You will sit a little higher than most other people driving SUV's and attract everyone's attention as you go by because of your noise and distinctive look. And, best of all, they will charge you at least $ 80k per copy, for a stripped down version, for the privilege of enduring all of the above.

Howard Schultz brought the high-end mentality to coffee. Starbuck's value proposition is that they will serve you a cup of very strong, mediocre coffee with exotic names for two to three dollars per cup. Furthermore, you have to call small—tall, large—grande, and extra large—ventee. If you don't they will smugly correct you and shout out the order using the right jargon as you slink over to the waiting counter under the scornful eyes of all the regulars who know that you really don't belong. The value proposition extends as they offer sofas, fireplaces, easy chairs, and computer kiosks to attract people to linger over their coffee and spend some time. Starbucks is in our face to be outlandishly trendy as much as Joe Willy Namath was in the face of every American in the 1960's as he strutted his stuff on Sundays and lived a publicly debauched life style that would have made Bill Clinton blush. And we loved him, as much as we love Starbucks today. It is their distinctive, differentiating value proposition.

What's yours?

Trait 6: Business Units Need to Understand and Leverage Business Synergies.

In theory, this one should be a no brainer. Business 101

would teach us that everyone working for a company ought to try to maximize profits for the company. Sub elements of the same company should not be working at cross-purposes with one another. A different discipline teaches us that "a house divided against itself cannot stand."

But let's say I'm the United States president, with NAFTA responsibilities, of a division of a large multi-national corporation based in Lucerne, Switzerland. My division manufactures specialty chemicals, and the other divisions of the company produce dyes and colorants, rubber, fibers, agricultural products, and agri-vet products. Although we have a North American headquarters located in Richmond, Virginia, where I report by dotted line, my annual evaluation is written by Dr. Peter Lanvan, my worldwide business director, in Lucerne with a dotted line to my CEO in Richmond. Dr. Lanvan expects me to maximize profits for my division to support his worldwide business needs. My U. S. boss expects me to contribute to the bottom line of the success of the North American business.

As is not uncommon in large corporations, three of our business groups sell to the same major customer. We each have our own sales and marketing folks, we each have our own travel budget, and we each have sales representatives making four to five sales calls per quarter on this client. How do we leverage the synergies between our various groups to make the most money for the company while serving the customer the best way we can?

Each group wants to maximize profits for his or her global business director. Each of us is under constant pressure to increase volume, increase sales, increase revenue & profit. Let's just say that I sell the most to this customer, about 700 million dollars in sales annually. Mendelson, who runs the rubber division, tells me he sells 100 million annually but the customer would up that to 500 million if I were willing to give the customer a price break on the chemicals I sell. Overall, we could increase North American revenue by about 350 million annually. Of course that means I would be reporting lower than forecasted earnings to my boss in Lucerne. He is not likely to look favorably on such a move. Who loses out? The company, of course! How do I leverage business synergies for the corporation's success?

In High Performance companies, employees, from senior executives to hourly operators, understand that they work for the company, not the region, division, or team.

Trait 7: Understand What it Takes to Transform an International Business into a Global Business.

There are many fine domestically run and multi-nationally led international businesses; there are precious few, truly global businesses. Being truly global involves much more than a geographical distinction or a matter of size or scope. It is a strategic business concept, a way of going to market, and a way of structuring the company's business model.

International businesses are headquarters centric. Major decisions are generated from Mortsel, Frankfurt, Quebec, Geneva, Minneapolis, Pittsburgh, Morristown, Bethesda, or Singapore. Global businesses are not headquarters centric; instead, the company leverages ideas domestically based on current and future best practices outside the domestic area. Business synergies are leveraged for the overall corporation not for individual strategic business units (SBU's) or geographical regions.

In a global corporation, helicopter vision is system wide. Those of you who have flown in helicopters know the difference between flying over Newark, New Jersey in a Continental MD 80 at 400 knots, and whoop, whoop, whooping over the Jersey City petroleum farms at 80 knots. In the jet you get a fairly limited view out your window. What you see is channeled to you based on the flight plan and the amount of Starbucks coffee consumed by the air traffic controllers. Stopping for a better look is not an option. In a helicopter, you can look left and right, up and down though clear panels in the floor. You can stop, hover, go back, and see the details if necessary. You have more control and better vision.

Global businesses pull this off by having people close to the action who understand the culture and language. They live there and don't try to run the business in India, China, and Vietnam from an office in downtown Sydney. They show up for meetings in Nairobi, Vientiane, Kinshasa, Cairo, Jakarta, and Madras as readily as those in Honolulu, Los Angeles, Hong Kong, and Long Boat Key, Florida. When they can't physically be present for the meeting they are linked 24x7x365 by VR technology putting major players together anytime anyplace in virtual meetings in innerspace. Because the best assets (managers, researchers, equipment, etc.) are not centered in the domestic head-quarters area, the company manages more effectively the know how of the global value chain.

Manufacturing sites are located around the world. These geographically diverse sites are run by local nationals, not by "foreigners" shipped in by the parent company. Because of the need to educate customers, employees, and suppliers around the world, the company spends a lot of time break-ing through cultural barriers by offering training in various languages. They create a global business culture by learning to value the mental models of diverse cultures. Diversity education is ongoing and ever changing. High performing global businesses constantly train in the areas of race, cul-ture, religion, gender, language, traditions, and ethnicity as they impact employees' perceptions and judgments. Expatriates are valued as resources, not coerced into getting "nationalized."

Most importantly, global businesses promote agile leaders who are capable philosophically, physically, and intellectu-ally of leading a diverse work force. The business battlefield in a global company is not comprised of the domestic one and all others. Assets must be deployed wherever necessary to dominate markets.

Trait 8: Have a Strong Sense of Identity.
On a daily basis, we are subjected to hundreds of commer-

cial messages. The desire always is to create a lasting impression on the customer. For most organizations this means that cultural branding must become pervasive. Both those inside and outside a company must come to identify the company with one mantra. Shelly Lazarus, CEO of Ogilvy and Mather, calls this a "core idea which the world can use. You find the universal" she says, "and then you make it the core of what you do."

Nothing runs like a... Deere.
Solutions for a small planet... IBM
The document company... Xerox
It's what's inside that counts... Intel
Federal Express: People, Service, Profits. Not only are the words important, but so is the order. If we put people first and give them the service they expect and require, the profits will come.

There are many cereals, but only one is "The Breakfast of Champions." There have been many detergents advertised over the years, but only one that my father knew was "99 and 44/100% pure." Only one soft drink is "misunderstood," only one vodka "leaves you breathless," only one candy (my favorite) "melts in your mouth not in your hand," only one toilet tissue is the "most squeezable product on the market," only one candy gives you "two great tastes in one," only certain toys "wobble but they won't fall down," and while they all are, most people think only one coffee "is mountain grown." These phrases may be merely the success stories of marketing firms, but the employees in these companies believe the hype, themselves. They all know these mantras, and so do you. They are part of their corporate visions. They have become part of our popular culture. That is 360 degree branding at its finest.

"I love what you do for me... Toyota!"

Or take a small entrepreneurial company in Indianapolis, Indiana who developed the website for my company, BitWise Solutions. Their mantra is "dream, develop, deliver." They do just that. And to be Internet visualization specialists on both a small and a large scale, the company needs all three elements there. They will succeed because they do what they proclaim. They *dream* with the client in their organizational "Greenhouse," they *develop* with the client by suggesting that the client move in with them in office space they will provide while the project is underway, and through collaborative thinking, they deliver. Their new Vertex C-Commerce tool fosters and facilitates collaborative project management allowing them to deliver from diverse geographical locations

For other companies, it means having a clear Purpose, Vision, Values, and Mission. These are statements and collections of values that define the culture of the organization. I will discuss these in much more detail in a later section.

It means, in short, that the company becomes a virtual living entity. I believe most companies have personalities, which can be as clearly described as an individual human personality. William Bridges offers one approach to understanding this living, breathing nature of the organization. His book, *The Character of Corporations,* is excellent in describing sixteen different organizational characters, related to the sixteen combinations of preferences identified by the Myers-Briggs Type Indicator®. When we work with companies to understand their character, we actually create a living organism, call it Swartz or Andrews, or Leshawn, or Wilson, who manifests all the personality traits that the organization does.

We ask seemingly silly questions like, if your company was a person:
1. Would it be male or female?
2. How would it dress on the job?
3. What would be its favorite song?
4. What would it do for fun?
5. What would be its favorite sport?
6. How many hours per week would it work?
7. How would it relate to the customer?
8. What kind of car would it drive?

9. What would its children say about it?
10. Where would it live? And many other questions designed to flesh out the essential character of the organization.

What surprises the company personnel is that this holographic representation of the organization culture is often far more than the personality of the CEO, the President, or the sum of the collective personalities of the employees. The company takes on a life—a personality—of its own. Once a company can identify its culture, it knows far easier how to market it—how to tell its story. The employees also become far more interested in keeping it alive.

Trait 9: Value Human and Physical Diversity.
This is one trait that, quite frankly, I was surprised to hear the corporate leaders assert as important. I always expect to hear senior leaders talk about the importance of diversity in their public pronouncements, but I am always pleasantly surprised to work with those leaders who actually passionately believe it. Steven Miller, beginning as the Group Managing Director at Royal Dutch Shell, and now a senior executive leading that company, wages an ongoing campaign to enhance and value workplace diversity. Helge Wehmeier, CEO of Bayer Corporation, is a highly principled leader who not only talks about diversity but also lives it! Colin Powell, both as Chairman of the Joint Chiefs of Staff under the elder Bush, Founder of America s Promise, and Secretary of State under George W. Bush, passionately believes it. Paul Galvin, CEO of Motorola, is another business leader who realizes that the "soft stuff" is the "hard stuff" for the future. Diversity is key to his creation of culture.

When Agfa Corporation, which at the time was still a division of Bayer Corporation, launched its diversity initiative in 1996, it was commissioned by a white, male, bachelor, German president named Erhardt Rittinghaus, who was passionate about changing the culture of his company. On the international side, the leadership of the Singapore government is, by far, the most diverse group of leaders with which I have ever worked. Where the surprise was for me was that the senior leaders we included in our discussion (leaders from Bayer, Agfa, Pfizer, PNC, Regions Bank, Eastman Kodak, J. C. Fuller, Harris Chemical, Allstates Trust Bank in Nigeria, AT&T, Marriott, and Millipore) brought up diversity **as a requirement for business high performance.** That was an exciting affirmation for me.

What has become clear over the years is that those companies that launch successful diversity education programs do so not because really nice, humanistic people lead them, but because their business leaders recognize diversity as a prudent business issue. What is quite obvious is that twelve middle-aged, pot-bellied white males in central Indiana might just not have a lot of insights into how to sell personal care products to African American females in South Central L. A. or multi-lingual Asians living in Singapore. Yet companies like Union Switch and Signal, Firestone, Genstar, Great Lakes Chemical, GRS, Texaco, Janus, Allied Signal, and others try it all the time. Diversity in these companies, when it exists, seems accidental and usually stays within the orbit of traditional white male leadership.

Diversity of people, thought, style, and opinion make up the culture that must be the infrastructure that supports business strategy. One more time:

Culture is the infrastructure that supports business strategy.

Trait 10: Measure what you claim is important.
This trait is one we find missing from many plans for achieving high performance. It is as simple as Sergeant Tootles' telling me 34 years ago, "Look, Lieutenant, the troops only do what the old man checks." At the geriatric age of 22, I was the "old man" back then. He was right then, and all the organizational gurus today who preach the need to check and set specific metrics, are just as on target.

Once we have a plan there must be specific goals, with definite time lines, with required outcomes established, or the organization will run amuck. Not because people will intentionally thwart the goals, but because things come up, people get sidetracked, and no one is checking on what is supposed to be done. The metrics may be financial, may be qualitative or quantitative, they may be as specific as the number of work orders completed in an 8-hour shift or as general as developmental goals for an individual over a year long period. The point is that we measure what we say we are going to do. I will measure subjective goals such as cooperation level on a team, and I will measure objective goals such as millions of square meters of products out the door. Once we know that a specific goal is required to satisfy a tactic that contributes to our strategy, I will track what the task is, who the person is who is responsible for the goal's completion, the time frame within which I expect the task completed, the actual time it is done, and, if possible, the cost required to complete the task. What helps the organization stay on track is to have several visual displays around the workplace that show what you are tracking.

Task	Due date	PPR	Completion Date	Cost
Mars Project	6/29/01	Martinez	6/17/01	1.3 mil
SAP, PH II	8/30/02	Schmitt		29 mil
Extruder inst	9/09/02	Crawford		est. 236 thou

Trait 11: Where Teams are Required, Train as Teams.
This one is not as simple as it sounds. Determining when a task requires a team and when it does not is often a leadership challenge. We banter about the word "team" these days to describe everything from a shift to a staff to a management group, to an intact work group. Our experience is that what passes for teams in most organizations is often little more than groups of people who are working together. Too often what gets sold as "team building" is little more than group building. Something dramatic has to

happen to transform a group into a team. It usually doesn't happen in a Holiday Inn between 8:00 am and 4:00 pm. Just as the Duke Blue Devils do not get to the Final Four by practicing two days a year, and the New York Yankees do not win the World Series by practicing once a month, so a business team does not create a winning organization without practice. Building a team takes time, and you have to know what you are trying to create before you begin.

When we are asked to help a group become a team, we prefer to take them off site and leave the cell phones and pagers behind. We will immerse the team in a series of action learning labs so members can practice the cognitive skills we discuss in the classroom. Recreation time during the training is also important, and we try to schedule at least a half-day of recreation for every three days we work. Some of the most valuable alliances are built on the golf course, tennis courts, skeet range, and hiking paths. The idea is to create a holistic model for team performance. You don't turn it on and off at the conference room door. Building a team becomes a way of life.

I recently agreed to a one-day, in-house team building session for a small high-tech company. Prior to the meeting, I met with the president to ascertain his desired outcomes and to discuss my plan for the day. I made it quite clear that the one-day session would lay the foundation for future work and would begin a process that he could pursue over the coming months. The session took place as scheduled. There was a lot of initial suspicion among the members of the company and some good healthy organizational paranoia regarding the president's motives. As the day proceeded the openness increased, and there was a lot of good-natured joking about individual preferences that had been discussed.

We closed the day with an electronic business simulation that involved two teams within the same company, each attempting to meet clearly defined goals with financial, scheduling, and quality parameters. The two teams immediately began to compete against one another, and the team on which the president was a member, heckled the other team the entire time and detracted from their performance and ability to meet the required parameters. Nothing unusual here; that is often the initial outcome of this particular simulation. While the directions are always given in a neutral fashion, organizations which have not practiced as teams always assume a competitive model. The simulation is designed to surface the very behaviors that occur in the office day after day. We finished off the day with a discussion of what had happened and why the two groups had acted as they had. One of the last comments I heard from one of the participants was, "so much for teambuilding!"

Indeed, "so much for teambuilding." If the team building had stopped here, it would have been a wasted day. In eight hours, the group had gone from a bunch of people who got along very politely and never confronted one another publicly when they disagreed—they just seethed quietly and complained to one another about the boss when he wasn't around—to a group willing to confront one another about significant problems in the workplace. They were willing to recognize significant differences among themselves and suddenly realized they were not of one mind about some significant issues. Indeed, after the one-day session two of the senior members of the organization took the president aside and discussed his behavior with him. I was present for this meeting and was pleasantly surprised by everyone's candor.

Two days later I got an e-mail and a telephone call from a senior vice president. The gist of his messages was, "the outcome from our session wasn't quite what I had hoped for. We are arguing with one another. It is not fun in the office right now." When I pressed him for details, he revealed that there had been a series of ongoing discussions and a slew of e-mails throughout the business about the session. Several people had been in to see the president about what had happened during the activity, and the COO and one other person had confronted the president about behaviors that were detrimental to the business's success. The VP wanted to know if this kind of outcome was normal.

I assured him that not only was such behavior normal, but it was predictable and desirable. I asked him if he had ever heard of Elizabeth Kübler-Ross's Five Stages of Grieving. He said he had, but it was just a model. The point, I assured him was that it is **just a model**, and many people choose to see it as just that until they suddenly lose a parent to a dreadful disease, watch an infant son die from an asthma attack, or go through a nasty divorce. Suddenly the model takes on a life of its own, and they will experience every one of the five stages, usually in the specific order described in *On Death and Dying*.

Teams also, I suggested, have a specific order of development. It is just a model until suddenly you find yourself going through the process. The model has been around for years and is usually known as the Four Stages of Team Growth: Forming ➡ Storming ➡ Norming ➡ and Performing. It was the natural, predictable transformation of this model that the organization was beginning to experience.

For years the organization had been in the Forming Stage. The president had been the founder and invested a lot of himself in the business—time, money, reputation, and family. There were times when he personally had taken no paycheck just to be able to meet the payroll during tough times. He had formed the organization and developed the initial model of how the company would develop. He had been successful and hired several people. There was probably a lot of pride, excitement, and anticipation about their future. While there may have been some suspicion and anxiety, people were proud of being chosen for the team, and there was some tentative attachment to what they thought of as their team. This is an exciting period in an organization's growth. I suggested that chances are that the vision and values I saw hanging on the wall when I came in were those of the president and he had, with all the best intentions, imposed them on the company. People were polite, they got along, they did their jobs, and no one really confronted anyone about issues when they arose. Such confrontations would be seen as disruptive of the harmony that existed.

What the organization will experience as a result of good initial teambuilding, I suggested, was the freedom to move to Stage 2. The president had taken the gutsy move to allow the company to begin teambuilding, and they had suddenly realized they had the freedom to disagree, to confront, and to challenge. Because we had begun with the MBTI® and had discussed the richness of personality preferences, the participants understood the source of some of their disagreements and had a model to confront them for the first time.

I assured the COO that the Storming Stage was the natural byproduct of good teambuilding when it is initially launched. Furthermore, if there is no Storming, there is no teaming. Oh, you might have a nice group without occasional conflict, but you will never have a team. Teams argue, confront, and fight, but they do it fairly and constructively. In Stage Two, there is some expressed reluctance to the task, sharp fluctuations in attitudes and arguing among members, even when they agree on the real issue. Factions oftentimes arise, and there can be defensiveness about one's position. There is a perceived pecking order and dissatisfaction with the hierarchy as well as unrealistic goals about how members should be working. Those in charge will be questioned as will the wisdom of putting certain people together on projects.

Welcome to genuine teambuilding.

This is the point to which the organization had arrived after the first session. Kudos to the president for taking the chance and making it happen. The company could have remained at the level of group for a long comfortable time and eventually suffered the fate of many of their dotcoms rivals—tombstones in the yellow pages and disconnected telephones.

Stage 3 is the Norming Stage. Here is where the real team-building work begins. The organization has to develop core values and operating principles—call these Norms—by which the team will hold one another accountable for living the values. It is a powerful stage and needs to be facilitated by a skilled team builder. Only then is the team capable of moving to the 4th Stage—Performing. Here is where the real results begin to be seen.

In the Performing Stage, team members begin to have insights into personal and group processes. Members understand one another's strengths and potential liabilities. Everyone learns how to leverage the intellectual capital of the individual members for team success. The team works through problems when they occur, they give and receive feedback honestly, they all become involved in continual learning, and they form close attachments to the team.

Forming, Storming, Norming, Performing. It is just a model, but every team goes through every stage. And, once the team begins to perform, every so often it slips back into Stage 2 and may have to revisit, and sometimes redefine, their norms.

Teambuilding never ends.

CHAPTER EIGHT

Up Close and Personal

From 30,000 feet, the Five Philosophical Underpinnings I discussed make great sense. Organizations need to understand these disciplines and develop them systematically to begin the journey to High Performance. With these five disciplines as the general framework, the traits of High Performing Corporations developed during our Conversations In Deer Valley come into stark relief. This 10,000-foot view of reality is attainable and measurable. We can work towards the eleven traits, and by monitoring the key metrics, we can determine when we are there. If we want to begin to make inroads into performance, however, we need to dip beneath the clouds and get down to the ground level. The way to hit the ground running is to look at the differences between traditional organizations—let's call them "groups" —and high performance organizations. For short hand, I'll refer to these, simply, as "teams."

A team is a group of common people who choose to direct their individual abilities and talents to work together on the basis of shared values toward a common vision in order to achieve uncommon organizational results.

That is what organizations want today—normal people, achieving abnormal results. Here are the differences.

Discussion vs. Dialogue
First Difference: Groups have discussions; teams involve people in dialogues. "Multilogues" would be better, but Dr.

Webster doesn't allow that one yet. Let's say you and I are having a discussion about the content of the new website for our pharmaceuticals division. I state my opinion to you, and you respond with your opinion. I hear the words coming out of your mouth, but instead of actually "listening" to them, I am in the process of reformulating to you my response. Ever do that? Welcome to the world of discussion. It is one sided and, at its heart, adversarial. Discussion always assumes, often subtlely and rarely articulated, that I know better than you. I listen to you almost as an inconvenience. This is discussion at its most puerile level. Sometimes it is less blatant but, nevertheless, just as stifling.

Walk into a meeting room and you can tell instantly the nature of the upcoming conversation. Are all the chairs facing in the same direction? Is there one chair up front facing your way? Is the podium facing your way? Are you sitting facing a flip chart or screen? Welcome to the world of discussion. You know going in that one person will be doing most of the talking and you will be doing the listening. It is the geometry of expertise that assumes that the one in front knows more than you. We expect this kind of arrangement when we are in a traditional learning environment, high school, college, professional school, but in the learning organization, we need to reconfigure the learning environment. Somehow the geometry must attract input from all the members of the team. Circles, squares, tables in rounds, or large open-ended U's are more effective.

Teams take time to practice giving and receiving feedback to one another. This is not a skill that comes easily or naturally to most people in the business world. It is a skill that can be learned, however. We encourage the teams we work with to develop skills using one or more of three "no-fault" feedback models. To be effective, feedback must be requested, clear, concise, and timely. "Oh, by the way, three weeks ago when you...." just doesn't cut it as meeting any of those four criteria.

How can feedback be "no-fault" ? We focus on describing a

behavior, stating the assumptions we make about the behavior, and relating how that interpretation of the behavior makes us feel. Any time we give feedback to another person, we are always revealing more about ourselves than we are the person to whom we are talking. The person always has the right to disagree with our interpretation of the behavior, just as we are always justified in rendering it. Once we work with teams on three variations of this model, we find that they routinely continue to use them back in the workplace.

Think about what happens in traditional labor negotiations. The union puts up the bargaining unit members at the Marriott Hotel, the management group stays at the Budget Inn, and the two groups travel to the Westin Conference Center for negotiation sessions. We walk into the room and the union sits at one side of a long table and the management sits at the other side. Welcome to the corrosive world of discussion. This is a classic, win-lose geometry that underscores the pitfalls of traditional negotiations. The session is doomed to arbitration at best and failure at worst. Once participants can learn and experience the advantages of a different model, for example that propounded by Principled or Mutual Gains Negotiations, drawing on the work done at the Harvard Kennedy School of Government and the Harvard Program For Negotiations, the geometry changes and so do the results.

When this same approach is taken into team meetings, staff meetings, or shift meetings, the model changes the results. The world of dialogue—multilogue—underscores the need to listen carefully to each member of the team. I will listen to you because I respect you and have learned to value your differences and the intellectual capital you bring to the job.

Most people are pretty bad about having dialogues in the workplace because they are bad at giving and receiving feedback. Folks don't offer feedback because it is perceived as meddling. At the same time, they don't request it because asking for assistance implies weakness. Sadly, these two poles also lead us into win-lose conversations that slide into one-sided discussion.

The Tolerance for Risk

Second Difference: Groups avoid risks; teams reward risks. Virtually every company we come across has a corporate value statement hanging on the conference room wall, printed on a wallet-sized card, or buried in pages of documents that includes as one of several values, the statement that "risk taking is valued." When we mention this value to the employees, we are always sure to generate a smile or a snicker. The smile speaks volumes. It tells us that the unspoken dependent clause is, "but don't screw up."

Many employees have seen people who take prudent business risks that succeed, and the person taking the risk is rewarded, sometimes monetarily, and occasionally substantially. But they have also heard about people who have taken such risks and fail, and the employees have departed suddenly. Which of the two consequences that occur, seems to be the luck of the draw? That, at least, is the story. Whether it is true or not is irrelevant. The perception that it is true is all that is necessary. It is a commonplace, but nevertheless true: perception is reality.

Human beings are smart, savvy critters. We sort options, we check out potential causes and effects, we look at the potential outcomes of our actions. We will work the pay off matrix pretty quickly. If the 4x4 matrix is as follows, the resulting actions are pretty clear.

Take a risk and succeed (reward)	Take a risk and fail (punished)
Don't take a risk. No success (no consequence)	Don't take a risk. No failure (no consequence)

If the only possibility in four for punishment follows from a person's taking a risk, and if there is no consequence for not taking a risk, you know which way the vote is going to be cast. People stop taking risks and nothing changes.

One of our clients in the midwestern part of the United States is in competition with a larger German corporation with which we have recently begun working. Both are in the specialty chemicals business, and both have been impacted by the ongoing implosion within the chemical industry. In both cases we work with them on their innovation pipeline. The German company has an average time from a new idea in an employee's mind to a new product on the market of four-five years. The American company has an average rate of 11 new products per year. If you were a venture capitalist, where would you invest? Nationality has little to do with the difference. There are as many slow and cumbersome North American companies as there are European ones. The difference is in the tolerance for risk and the extent to which the companies have become risk averse or nurtured a culture of prudent risk taking.

Walk into the U. S. company on four Fridays a year, and you will likely find one or two people wearing t-shirts proudly announcing, "I Blew Ten Grand Last Quarter!" The company is not frivolous, reckless, or irresponsible. It is, however, passionate about rewarding individuals for acting on ideas and creating profitability. They hold quarterly failure parties to celebrate employees who took a prudent business risk that should have worked but for whatever reason it bombed.

If a company only rewards success and condemns failure, not much new and exciting happens.

Now, I am not suggesting you go into the t-shirt business, and I know in most companies if you bragged even once that you had blown "Ten Grand" it would not be a cause for celebration. I am suggesting, however, that every company that strives towards High Performance needs to create some safety nets for failure. Sometimes, the net is simply a fostered team mentality that says, "It's our fault." Not John, not Elizabeth, not Shawnee, but us. We stop blaming others, and the team assumes ownership. The 3M Company learned many years ago that if they only rewarded successes and condemned failures, there would not be a lot of 3M Post-it Notes hitting the market.

The Focus of Competition

Third Difference: Groups compete internally, against each other; teams compete externally. Different cultures have very different views about the value of competition. A child who grows up in Japan, for example, learns from the earliest years that competition is bad and cooperation is good. Much of their time in the early years of school is spent learning how to give a proxy of their will to the group. Children learn not to seek self-aggrandizement. As long as the group succeeds, the individual succeeds. Consequently, building teams within the Japanese culture is an easier assignment than building teams in most western cultures.

Americans thrive on competition and too often breed it in our children from the earliest age. Listen to the conversations on the sidelines of youth soccer games or Little League Baseball games: get 'em, kill 'em, shoot it yourself, take it into the goal, take her out! When Paul's team loses, we console him. "That's ok, you'll do better the next time. Hey, you played a good game. The team just lost." When his team wins, it's high five time! Let's stop at the Dairy Queen on the way home and celebrate the win with a chocolate-chip-cookie-dough Blizzard. You would never hear these conversations in many other countries. I am not making a value judgment; I am just stating a fact.

In recent years a swarm of do-gooders and consultants have descended on the U. S., like a plague of locusts, trying to weed out competition. One of our kids currently attends a prestigious Jesuit high school where they do not rank order the children and have no Valedictorian or Salutatorian because doing so breeds competition. Nonsense! They do not deserve our money. The school is preparing the kids for the Garden of Eden not the real world. Wait until those deluded kids get into the business world or the military service and expect the same coddling.

A yuppie community near our town, let's name the culprit—Carmel, Indiana—had a silent soccer day last year, during which the parents could not cheer for their children because doing so, they claimed, breeds competition, potential violence among competitive parents, and the wrong values. This year, every soccer day in that community is a silent day. Parents in many communities have to sign a pledge prior to little league season saying they will be peaceful and respectful. If they do not sign the pledge, the kids can't play. I have warned our kids; if that ridiculous, benighted program ever comes to Zionsville, Indiana, my kids are finished with youth league soccer, and I will never coach another team. If we ever play Carmel on silent Saturday, they will need someone with a uniform and a badge dragging my cheering body off the soccer field in front of as many TV cameras as I can assemble. I am sure some Amendment covers that issue.

In short, now that the emotional diatribe has ended, I will match my competitive nature with anybody, anytime. I just want to know against whom I am competing? West Point did not develop someone who revels in ties. When I compete, I compete to win. Competition is not the issue. Where most organizations err is in breeding competition between the wrong parties. Business units compete against each other for funding or scarce resources. We compete for R&D funds, we compete for budget approval and funding for capital expenditures. Many five-day budget allocation meetings in large corporations are uglier than food fights at Delta Tau Delta.

Some manufacturing sites I have worked with encourage shifts to compete against each other in order to increase productivity. So what happens is, A shift leaves the work area dirty so B shift has to clean up before they begin. B shift fails to call in a work order on the mixer that went down just before the shift ended so C shift can't out produce them, and D shift has to report a near miss in their safety record, because an over zealous employee hurts herself trying to fix the broken mixer so the shift doesn't fall behind in its production goals once again, while they wait for centralized maintenance to respond to their problem. What a naive understanding of human nature. This practice is a dinosaur of the business world and the quicker to the tar pits the better.

High Performance organizations foster a competitive spirit—competition contributes to high performance—but they teach organizations the appropriate locus of the competition. High Performance Corporations focus the competition externally, against the "COMPETITION" as Business 101 describes them. There should be no competition within!

The Nature of the Agenda

Fourth Difference: Groups have individual agendas; teams have a team agenda. The fourth follows the third difference not only because numerical sequencing demands it but also because they are closely linked. You have all been part of a cross functional group that has been chartered to research and make recommendations about a major issue facing the company. There are representatives from finance, human resources, marketing, and R&D. Two senior sales reps have been assigned to the group as well as three managers from manufacturing and one from customer service. The designated group leader is a manager who has recently been reengineered out of a job, so now he is the special projects manager. The first few meetings go rather smoothly, as people are getting to know each other and acting cordially.

Increasingly, however, the group fails to reach any consensus. The sales reps argue with the marketing manager about her last marketing campaign. The customer service representative tries to mediate the discussions and is shut down by sales because their customers are ticked off by an unresponsive ordering system. Manufacturing thinks they are all living in a dream world. Finance says there is no new money available, and the human resources representative is dinged for launching a diversity initiative and a new benefits package while the company is struggling to meet sales quotas. The special projects manager just finished managing the SAP project, so everyone really appreciates him! So he hires a consulting company to come in to give two days of classes on conflict management before the whole projects goes belly up.

In a typically silo-structured organization, turf is always the primary agenda. No group can come together to solve collective problems as long as the silo is the dominant force. As long as I represent sales or marketing or manufacturing, that functional entity will presuppose my fealty. In organizations which are rigidly structured along functional lines, when groups come together for company-wide issues they must begin by creating a unified charter for the efforts underway. They must understand their mission, their goals, and the common values to which they are willing to hold one another accountable. They must create a Team Agenda to which they are all obligated, and this agenda must be communicated to the organization as a whole so there are no hidden agendas suborning the process.

Many years ago when General Alexander Haig was the SACEUR (The Supreme Allied Commander Europe), he caught a lot of grief from the American press as well as senior U. S. military officers for not supporting U. S. interests clearly enough. They were arguing from inside the U. S. silo, which was only one among many in the alliance. Haig's agenda was the NATO agenda that said his job was to act in the best interests of the alliance, even if that might go against U. S. interests from time to time. Because he carried out that task in such a value-centered way, he remains today, in the eyes of the European allies, the most highly thought of American ever to have held that position.

Perhaps nowhere in business is it more important to establish a "team agenda" than during times of merger and acquisition. The grand failures over the last decade cry out for a strategy between would-be partners to avoid making the mistakes of the past. Often mergers are like third and fourth marriages—triumphs of hormones and hope over history and experience. AT&T's 1991 disastrous acquisition of NCR took years to ameliorate. Compaq's 1998 takeover of Digital destroyed both companies. There are fortunately also some success stories such as the 2000 merger between America On Line and Time Warner, McDonnell Douglas' merger with Boeing, Citibank's merger with Travelers to form Citigroup, and Chrysler's merger with Daimler-Benz. But in every case, one culture wins out over the other. As the joke in the industry goes, there is no doubt in anyone's mind that in Germany, the new Daimler-Chrysler Corporation is pronounced Daimler.

Increasingly, we hear the term merger of equals bantered about to describe a coming together of two corporations for their mutual good. Despite the smiles and the handshakes as the merging leaders ring the bell to open the trading on Wall Street, there is no such thing as a "merger of equals," regardless of what the pundits call it. It's George Orwell's *Animal Farm*, all over again; some pigs are more equal than others. In a merger of equals, one culture is more equal than the other, and it will always emerge as dominant, even if the due diligence does not predict it. In an acquisition, it is always easy to view one company as the conquering hero whose job it is to shape up the losing, acquired company, and the games begin.

In the early 1990's I was working with a German-owned manufacturing site that was acquired by a Belgian-parented, U. S. company. The acquired plant manager, an Austrian by birth, made it known throughout his plant that even though they had been acquired and the name outside the plant had changed, they would never be part of the new company. He made it his personal agenda to undermine every effort at assimilation and culture change. It took four years for the acquiring company to realize the disastrous impact of his culture war. His removal was required before the site could ever begin to be assimilated into the new company.

In the aftermath of the September 11, 2001 terrorist attack on the United States, strident individual agendas began collapsing into one collective agenda to combat global evil. In the United States, Democrat and Republican leadership of the Congress sang "America The Beautiful" on the steps of Congress; in the weeks following, they spoke with one accord refusing to be torn apart by partisan politics. Pakistan, India, Russia, the Sudan, and other countries never aligned with the United States offered assistance in tracking down the killers and those who assisted them. The power of a unified agenda can overwhelm opposition.

Here in Indiana, farmers are the arbiters of cultural wisdom. As my corn-raising neighbor reminds me from time to time, "If you chase two rabbits, both will escape." Nowhere is that more evident than in the rice bowl mentality that persists among the various intelligence services in the United States. Governor Tom Ridge, newly appointed cabinet head of Homeland Defense, has as his major task the elimination of separate agendas and the formulation of a team agenda to ensure the kinds of intelligence lapses that may have helped facilitate the events of 911 never occur again. For years the firewalls between the CIA, FBI, NSA, NRO, local police forces and Interpol have been so thick that any necessary intelligence tips were rarely shared. Compartmentalization prevented collaboration.

Hesitancy vs. Openess
Fifth Difference: Groups practice hesitancy; teams practice openness and trust. This difference explains the quality of discourse in senior staff meetings, team meetings, town meetings, and feedback sessions across the organization. Watch the body language and listen to the topics discussed and the depth to which they are discussed. Traditional organizations are very polite. People treat one another cordially and never act rudely in public. In meetings, participants "check" what they say. They are not dishonest and do not "not tell the truth," they just tell partial truths. They save the whole truth for the bar, the pizza shop, the break

room, or the smoke shack. There is this pervasive myth that holds that telling the truth might cause controversy or conflict, so we are hesitant to tell the whole truth in meetings.

High Performing organizations have learned that teams have conflict; groups don't. In a similar vein, if you do not have conflict in your relationship from time to time, you have a dead relationship. But that's a different book. Teams have conflict. It is just that in teams, members have learned that conflict is merely creative tension. One person is at position A and the other is at position E. We need to find a more creative way than we have so far of moving A and E together, maybe at position K. We prematurely narrow our options and erroneously assume there are only two options when there might actually be seven. Good conflict management requires trained innovative thinkers to break through the blocks to innovation and creativity and see new ways of working together.

Sometimes, people will say, but Bill, you have to understand, we have "irreconcilable differences—IRRECONCILABLE!" That to me is a meaningless statement. In my company over half of my consultants are female, and three are African American. I am male, and white. These differences—despite medical wonders today—are irreconcilable. I will never be a black female. Does that mean we can't work together? Of course not! Irreconcilable differences are meaningless. What we must work on day-by-day is creating an environment of openness and trust. Openness and trust win over hesitancy and checking every time.

Availability of Information
Sixth Difference: Groups file information; teams share it. If you have read Taming the Scorpion, this story will sound suspiciously familiar, but it bears retelling. When I left West Point as a young second lieutenant on the way to Vietnam at least once and probably more, one learning that was instilled in me by officers and non-commissioned officers alike was that I needed to pay attention to my sergeants. They had "been there and done that." I would be

wise to heed their advice. My first assignment before heading to Southeast Asia for my first tour was at an artillery base in Balesfeld, Germany. There I met Sergeant Lacy Carmack, my platoon sergeant. He had been the acting platoon leader for a number of months and knew my job as well as his inside and out.

Early in our relationship Carmack said, "Lieutenant, I have some advice for you." He wasn't always so blunt, so I figured it must be pretty valuable advice. "What's that, Sergeant Carmack?" I queried. "Lieutenant, you never tell the troops everything. Because if you do, they won't need you any longer." Now, I must admit, that did not sound right, but I was new and he was the old hand, so I tentatively tried out his advice. I'd give Sgt. Mullen his bit of information, SSG, Tuddy his piece of the information, SSG Martinez his piece, and SSG White his little piece. Meanwhile, I'd keep the big picture for myself. That way I knew I was the boss. It made me feel important.

About a week later, Carmack said, "Lieutenant, are you a red rock lieutenant or a white rock lieutenant?" I figured it was one of those tricks NCOs play on junior officers to trick them up, so I asked him what he meant. "Well," he said, "the last platoon leader we had made us paint all the rocks in the company area, white. The officer we had before him, had us paint all the rocks, red. What color do you want them? Rock painting stopped that day in Balesfeld, Germany and so did paying attention to everything Carmack said. And that is exactly what he wanted to happen, because Carmack was a savvy leader and a great mentor. He knew I would have to learn these things on my own.

In that teaching moment, Carmack was able to impart the entire history of the leadership vacuum his platoon had suffered under for the previous six years. He and his platoon had been subjected to micromanagement, debasement, and the abuse of information for years. Micromanagers "file" information; leaders "share" it. I very quickly learned that I needed to share as much information as possible as soon as possible, because in that business, I might have been dead the next minute.

In the business world, employees sadly have learned the same behavior. In an environment where right-sizing and down-sizing have become the norm, not the exception, people play it safe. Employees watch supervisor after supervisor withhold information, piecemeal data out to employees, and micromanage others in an effort to protect themselves in the next inevitable purge. After all, if I know more than you, when it comes time to pick you or me to go, I have the edge. High performers share information and contribute to the overall learning of the organization in the process. Information is always power, but in an information age,

information is a critical strategic resource.

Not Failing vs. Succeeding

Seventh Difference: Groups focus on Not Failing; Teams focus on Succeeding. Our clients tell us that this one is the most important of the baker's dozen. I think they are all important; but this one gets the highest reviews in terms of being a powerful distinction that employees can readily understand.

Human beings are story-telling creatures. As early as Homeric bards singing the glories of heroes and the peccadilloes of the gods and goddesses, or primitive peoples drawing pictures on the walls of caves and dwellings we have communicated important events with stories comprised of pictures. Much of our research on the brain tells us we store brain contents in chemical and electronic pictures. All of us are capable of creating mental pictures of various kinds.

Take just a minute or two and create what for you would be a mental picture of succeeding. What does success look like for you? For one of my colleagues, Jerry, success might be teeing off on a par three at Fiddler's Elbow Country Club in New Jersey and watching that little white ball leave the head of his five iron and sail 175 yards and bury itself in the hole for his third hole-in-one this year—a clear picture of success. For Jeff, success might be seeing one of his stocks he bought at four dollars a share, get hyped on CNN Market Watch and soar to 43 dollar a share by the close of the market. Success for Leah might be winning her age group in the Shamrock Marathon. Success for me might be seeing my son Paul at high school graduation running up and giving me a huge hug and saying, "Thanks Dad. I couldn't have done it without you." Who wouldn't want that picture? Maybe success for you is seeing yourself win the Chairman's Award at the next leadership meeting or seeing yourself named as the new Chairman of the Board. Our pictures are all different, but we can all create them.

We can also create for ourselves a picture of failure. It's fairly easy to do. If you watched television with me on Sunday or Saturday afternoon during the 1960's, you saw week in and week out, *the thrill of victory and the agony of defeat.* We watched dozens of times as that poor guy zipped down the ski jump, fell off, and crashed head over teakettle again and again and again. A clear-cut picture of failure!

We can create a picture of "succeeding," and we can create a picture of "failing." What we cannot create is a picture of "not." Can't do it! The mind will always put something there. What that means is that if I take my 35mm camera and aim it at a picture of "succeeding" and push the shutter, I am going to get a picture of SUCCEEDING. If I aim that same camera at a picture of "not failing," what am I going to get a picture of? I'll get a picture of FAILING, because I can't see the "not." What are you focused on in your business: succeeding or not failing? If you are focused on succeeding, you are on an exciting path towards High Performance. You will achieve success. If, on the other hand, you are focused on not failing, you will most likely fail, because the "not" is not in your vision.

Despite my several years as an English professor, this distinction is far more than a matter of word choice or language. The distinction conveys an entirely different philosophical approach to the mission. Listen to the language used in your organization. If you have a new product being launched, a new marketing campaign beginning, or a merger underway, what are employees saying about the importance of the project. If the language is "we dare not fail," "we better not fail," "we can" t afford to fail on this one," the company is in serious trouble. I guarantee you, in your relationships, in your business, in your partnerships, or in your mergers, you will get whatever you focus on. The vision is critical.

The Nature of Hierarchy

Eighth Difference: Groups have an obtrusive hierarchy; teams have a transparent hierarchy. By hierarchy, I do not mean to imply merely the complexity of the wiring diagram that describes the company's organization. At stake is the ease by which information is generated and transferred up, down, and throughout the organization. I have worked with some companies that are more stratified and more buttoned down than the U. S. Marine Corps. They wouldn't think about calling the president by his first name, and they wouldn't know what to wear if they had a casual Friday, but they transfer information, they delight the customer, and they exceed shareholder expectations.

And then there are those companies that by all the external trappings look open and communicative, but which are wracked by bickering, infighting, a lack of cooperation, and stove-piped communications systems. Everybody is on a first name basis across the organization, but there is no culture to support the infrastructure of the organization, and, therefore, nothing gets communicated.

Some of my favorite groups to work with are the elite special operations teams around the world: the SAS (the British commandoes known as the Special Air Services), Delta Force (the U. S. hostage rescue unit), German GSG9 (a super secret hostage rescue unit), Seal Team 6, and an unnamed group in Israel. In garrison, they can all be spit and polish. They don't like it, but they can pull it off. Line up twelve of them at Dam Neck, Virginia, or in "the other compound" at Fort Bragg, North Carolina, and you can tell by looking at them who outranks whom. But when they go to the field, when they go "operational," when they meet **their** customers, you have a hard time telling who the lowest ranking non commissioned officer or the most senior officer is. All you know is that whoever has the clearest picture of what the customer needs, is in charge. They will direct the team. Hierarchies become transparent when the constant learning of the company reinforces the frame of mind that every employee, every day, constantly asks, "how, is what I am doing right now, directly impacting the customer?"

The information available to us today is so voluminous that no one can ever again control the whole organization from one desk in Wayne, New Jersey; one desk in West Lafayette, Indiana; or a corner office in Oakland, California. Transparency means information flows up, down, and across with alacrity and ease.

Information vs. Process Orientation

Ninth Difference: Groups have an information orientation; Teams have a process orientation. This one is easy to spot. Let's go to your management team meeting. What does the agenda look like, and what is discussed? Too often the members spend the bulk of their time updating each other on what has gone on in their specific functional area of expertise since the last meeting. The CFO goes over the P&L, and the same division VP's that got hammered last meeting get nailed again. Human Resources discusses the incentive plan and the training initiatives underway, there is a special report from the ESHA manager, and the legal counsel updates the group on the due diligence underway. Everybody not under attack is yawning and wondering why they bothered to fly in for the meeting. What a pathetic use of highly paid people's time and talent!

With all the capability we have today to communicate and share information, this process should occur before the meeting. Teams that still use in-person meetings to "share" information are dinosaurs in the modern age. Meetings should be used to challenge, change, create, plan, and innovate—"process," if you will.

Control vs. Inclusion

Tenth Difference: Groups emphasize control; teams emphasize inclusion. I remember a fifty-year-old supervisor at BART (the Bay Area Rapid Transit system), saying to me one time in a session I was holding on High Performance in the Oakland Raiders Conference Room, "Look, Jeffries, I have spent my entire career making it to this level. I am finally here with the title of supervisor, and I'm in charge. I like that, and now, because of guys like you, the organization expects me to give up all of that control." And, if he believes that sentiment, he is absolutely right. Remember, during times of change, people will perceive change as loss. "Look what I am losing now," was his complaint.

What this distinction really points out is the difference between "doing it **to** somebody," versus "doing it **with** somebody." Team performance emphasizes involvement rather than exclusion. I am not asking him to give up anything; rather, I am asking him to increase his personal power and influence by working with others. This change in approach requires substantial re-training.

This particular fifty-year-old supervisor speaks for thousands of supervisors and middle managers who have been left out in the major reengineering efforts that radically changed the work force during the 1990's. It is this group, more than most, who find themselves caught in the middle. Supervisors are considered to be the enemy by those beneath them because they are imposing all the changes, and they are seen as the problem by senior leaders for not "getting on board" and acting decisively to work themselves out of jobs. They are "the excluded middle," and must be schooled and retrained as coaches, facilitators, resources, or leaders in the new work place or they will sabotage (consciously or unconsciously) the entire change effort. If your organization is going through major transitions and you have not planned for at least three-five days for retraining your middle managers and supervisors, you are flirting with disaster.

Values

Eleventh Difference: Groups sometimes have individual values; teams always have common values. Many years ago, when I was a full time English professor, I was active in many associations concerned with pedagogy, curriculum content, and educational reform. I was usually a thorn in the side of most of these organizations because I believe in teaching values in public as well as private schools. In fact, from my perspective, there is probably nothing more important to teach. Any time the word "values" comes up in connection with teaching, every special interest group in the world digs down into their coffers to find a way to shut you up, and those in charge find a way to remove you. "Whose values are you going to teach? Who is to say what is right or wrong?"

The problem of course content and what values should be taught is solved in our founding documents. The values are not those found in a particular religion or sect. I, as an American citizen, have a rich heritage of values handed down to me in the country's founding documents. Public education has an obligation to teach these values found in the Constitution, Declaration of Independence, and Bill of Rights. They are the heritage that provide the values and sub strata to be a mature citizen. They are the values that made this country the adopted home of so many people from other rich cultures and backgrounds. They are the values which make us the target of hatred and terrorism by many radical groups around the world. Sadly, many Americans don't even know what values these documents affirm. They are our culture's philosophical presuppositions. They are the starting point, and our schools should teach them unapologetically!

I was debating one college president—a self-proclaimed expert in educational ethics—at a historic ivy-covered university in the northeast (in Boston, on the river) when he began to sing the virtues of a values-neutral curriculum. When I asserted that a values-neutral environment was itself a value, he seemed nonplussed. And he should have been perplexed, because teaching in a values-neutral environment can't be accomplished. When you preach a "values-neutral" education, what you tell students is that values are irrelevant and need not be considered in arriving at conclusions regarding our system of government, scientific research on the environment, economics, social sciences, stem cell research, comparative world literature, the terrorist attack on the World Trade Center and the Pentagon, and anything else they might study. That ethical void is frightening and can lead to moral anarchy.

Let's go to your organization. All of us have individual values, things we hold dear, principles we live and die by, issues for which we will go to bat. Some may be traditional and some may be more avant-garde. Some of you spent your youth as an altar boy, some spent it in the Girl Scouts, and others spent it at Woodstock. Some of you may have taken a Girl Scout to Woodstock. For some of you, Lenny Bruce is your culture hero, and for others it might be Malcolm X or Mother Teresa. We all value-processed at different shrines. These diverse sources all spawned different values.

When we do executive coaching we spend a good bit of time looking at the values that inform who we are and how we act. Invariably some executive tells me, "Look, Bill, I have very clear values. Do you want me to tell you what they are?" My answer is invariably, "no." "But, I'll tell you what," I responded, "if you show me your Franklin Planner and your checkbook, I will tell **you** what your values are." It's where you spend your time and money that your values reside. Where do you spend your time and money? What do your children see? What do your employees see?

Where does your company spend its time and money? What are the shared values that your customers, suppliers, and employees know you stand for, and to which you are willing to be held responsible? This is the important question with which teams begin.

Diversity

Twelfth Difference: Groups accept differences; teams value diversity. We are finally getting to the place where the first independent clause in that statement is more or less expected in the workplace. Some companies are still proud, however, to tell me they "accept diversity." Some print it proudly in their value statement. My response is usually, "big deal!" Accepting diversity is analogous to admitting, "well there are more of them than there are of me these days, so I guess we better accept diversity." It is not unlike General Custer accepting the fact that he will not win at Little Bighorn.

I can make anyone "accept" diversity; it is a simple legal issue. I hold you accountable in your annual evaluation or tie part of your incentive package to accepting diversity. You can watch an organization turn on a dime when that happens. Ernie Drew, as the CEO of Hoechst Celanese did that back in the early 90's. He mandated values, and the company changed swiftly. I didn't particularly care for his style or some of his values, but he was effective in establishing certain core values in the company. Until the mandate evaporated, under new management in the mid 1990's, Hoechst Celanese was one of the most value-centered companies I knew.

Valuing diversity is a whole different issue. It is a moral one. I can mandate acceptance. I have to educate, coach, and train towards valuing.

The Myth of Empowerment

Thirteenth Difference: Groups are directed; teams have become empowered. During the 1970's and '80's "quality" was the catchword. Everyone was sent to quality seminars based on systems created by Juran, Crosby, or Deming. In the 1990's, "team" became the *program de jour*, and everyone thought they had to build teams for every task, even those where a plain old group and sometimes an individual might do just fine. If you weren't talking "teams" you were not considered cutting edge. The calendar page turned, and now empowerment is the myth of the third millennium. Everyone wants to become empowered, and employers want empowered work forces. The problem is that no one can empower anyone to do anything!

Empowerment is a personal choice.

You can't get empowered by running off to the local Holiday Inn to attend a Career Tracks seminar for ninety-five bucks and sit there filling in a notebook for seven hours. You don't empower a group by hiring DDI to present one of their canned presentations on empowerment, and you sure don't get empowered by watching Tony Robbins or Fran Tarkington spewing out platitudes in their early morning infomercials. Tony Robbins' inner giant may have empowered him, but I'll take Shrek any day over him. Each person must choose to become empowered. If you are waiting to be empowered by someone you work for, you will wait until dinosaurs roam your headquarters again. Empowerment is a personal choice, and no amount of training or schooling will provide it for you.

If you are in charge, you can enable you employees to become empowered by doing your job. What's your job? What is your task as a leader? Every book has a different definition, but for me,

leadership is the ability to help organizations and individuals surpass themselves.

It is, therefore, a great metaphor for an age where businesses are always expected to do more with less. Rather than recite a laundry list of leader responsibilities, let me suggest you can boil down the bulk of a leader's time to three responsibilities. Leaders should:

1. Speak the vision,
2. Live the Values, and
3. Remove the Obstacles.

That is a full time job for most of us.

Everywhere a leader goes, employees ought to hear the leader articulating the corporate vision, the company vision, or the team vision. Employees should get sick and tired of hearing the vision again, and again, and again. Of course you have to have one to articulate it, and it needs to be succinct and memorable enough for employees to get it. When Susan walks into the break room for third shift and her team can be heard saying, "uh oh, here she comes; we are going to hear the vision for the hundredth time," then she is actually starting to communicate it enough. Leaders speak the vision, speak the vision, speak the vision!

Secondly, leaders have to live the values. Of course we have to have them to live them—check out your personal day planner and check book—but the leader must exemplify the values the team says are important. Regardless of whether leaders are introverts or extraverts, they must be willing to live in glass houses. They should be clear in their desire to be held responsible by others for the values they affirm.

Thirdly, leaders have to spend the bulk of their time removing the obstacles so others can get their work done. Sometimes the obstacles are old equipment that needs to be replaced, sometimes the obstacles are old legacy systems that need to go away, sometimes the obstacles are people who simply **will not change;** they hurt others and business performance. There are times when those people need to go.

What we find is that if leaders will speak the vision, live the values, and remove the obstacles, those who work for them will choose to become empowered. It is a personal choice.

CHAPTER NINE

Making it Happen in Your House

Look around the business world today, in your peer group and elsewhere. Who do you look to as a model of success? One of the dilemmas I have as I read the business gurus touted over the last few years as business experts is the success stories they discuss in their books. Tom Peters, Peter Senge, Marvin Weisbord, Stephen Covey, Geary Rummler, Ken Blanchard, and others cite example after example in their books of successful companies which have ceased to exist or floundered before the book goes into paperback. Who are you to believe? Today's hero is tomorrow's dog.

In the 1990's, pundits were praising Robert Shapiro, the CEO of Monsanto, for his insight, vision, and gospel of corporate responsibility. He was years ahead of other corporate leaders investigating the possibilities of cutting-edge genetic research. He saw Monsanto's motto, "food, health, hope" as the perfect vehicle for applying molecular research to agriculture and pharmaceuticals. I always saw him as a visionary genius. Then, beginning with the merger between Monsanto and Pharmacia & Upjohn things started going south very quickly. Today, depending who you talk to, Shapiro was either a forward-thinking leader who revolutionized agribusiness or a naive bungler who misread the European culture and was unable to extricate Monsanto before it became too late. His, was the potential fate of every legitimate visionary.

It is easy enough to look at the 2001 decline in the NAS-DAQ and attack the business model used by the dotcoms and the over exuberance of a generation of investors who didn't see a decline in their IRA's for seventeen years for some of the mess in which the high tech businesses find themselves. But what are we to make of the huge decline in the DOW and the over production of the industrialized companies? Why are they facing stagnation? Why does a star like Lucent Technologies dive from $ 85 / share to $ 6 / share and talk of bankruptcy? Why is ISP's stock in perpetual single digits? Why does a company like Great Lakes Chemical, in which Warren Buffet is so highly invested, repeatedly turn in lower than predicted profits and dividends? Why are major pharmaceutical companies down by a third in their stock price?

Why is the chemical industry worldwide facing the same bleak future that the domestic steel industry confronted twenty years ago? Today, chemicals are in the same fix steel found itself two decades ago—consolidation and then complete neglect. We have heard about one major acquisition after the next. The industry consolidates, companies grow larger, diversity education, leader development, quality training, and team building are all eliminated in favor of SAP and removing costs from processes. Everything they learned when they were smaller got left behind when they grew larger. Steel went belly up, and the industry moved to Japan, Russia, and Latin America. The chemical industry faces the same potential fate today.

In the case of many of these companies, the failure and stagnation were caused by an absolute void of enlightened leadership and excessive micromanagement. When one looks at the existing senior leadership of some of these companies, it is not surprising to see them doing as badly as they are. But what about other well-publicized failures such as Jack Welch's global missteps in the biggest acquisition of his distinguished career, Jill Barad's beleaguered tenure leading Mattel, Inc., or the meltdown at MicroStrategy, Inc. presided over by the visionary CEO Michael Saylor? What of the failure of the United Airlines / U. S. Airways Merger, or Robert Shapiro's failure at Monsanto to understand the European view of genetically altered products? Why did the Board of Directors of Hewlett-Packard have to declare their public support for Chief Executive Carly Fiorina, in August 2001, in an effort to end the speculation that she would be dismissed because of a continued slump in profits; all this just a month before she was named the new CEO of the HP acquisition of Compaq. Will she leave a legacy of success or be held up as a corporate scapegoat when the deal folds? Why can't Chairman and Chief Executive Officer Henry Schacht of Lucent Technologies put together a strategy capable of saving the rapidly expiring communications giant?

Why are so many potentially powerful companies in the dumpster?

More importantly,

How do clever, experienced leaders craft such business disasters?

In some cases the failure is the consequence of the triumph of marketing over business—of hype over substance. Many leaders because of their egos, their distrust of vision, their myopic approach to long-term issues, and their fear of the analysts craft their companies for short term successes and long term failure. Often, it is just plain greed. The vision is the dollar, nothing more. While this is not a leadership book, it is a book about leaders and what leaders do. Leaders craft their organizations for success. High Performing leaders:

1. Have highly developed interpersonal skills,
2. Keep an eye on the task at hand,
3. Develop good communication skills,
4. Grow replacements by teaching them the business,
5. Set high expectations of themselves and others,
6. Model the behaviors they expect of others,
7. Mentor others and seek personal mentoring,

8. Listen before they speak,
9. Read voraciously and surf the web frequently, and
10. Build High Performing Leadership Teams and practice over and over.

The question is, where do you begin? It won't happen automatically, and there is no short cut. How do you start to create a High Performing Leadership Team? You put into place a plan to create Systematic Organizational Mastery. Regardless of whether a person is working on an elite military team or a highly productive business team, the principles are the same. You can implement them in your organization immediately.

Identifying Your Purpose
We begin by asking you to identify your purpose.
Why do you exist as a staff, group, team, or business entity?

The answer ought to be clear and easily identifiable. If it is not, that is a bad sign.

Were you chartered into existence by another organization; if so, what does the charter say? What are you expected to deliver?

Has your group simply always been there and, therefore, it is assumed you must have a purpose?

What has it done in the past?

Is it still necessary?

Were you just promoted to President and inherited a management group with the job?

Who is on that staff?

Should they be there?

Do they add value?

Whom do you serve (both internally and externally)?

We are constantly amazed at the groups and teams with whom we work that cannot answer these simple questions. I am frequently contacted to "do some team building," and when I ask "to what end," the group is stumped. They manage to stammer out something like, "work together better, be more productive, be a better model, get along better, handle conflict better," or the like. But to what end, is the question. Why do you exist? Just to make money is insufficient. Greed is not a vision. Once the group knows why it exists and can articulate a clear purpose for their existence, it is ready for the first important collaborative task.

Creating Common Values
The group must identify its common values that they are willing to act on consistently. The key words are "common" and "consistently." Values are the bedrock of any culture and, as the essence of that culture, they provide a common vector that all employees can see and follow. Because values shape our actions, they should be made tangible so the entire organization knows what distinguishes the group from the rest of the organization, and if they are company values, they must declare the core principles that make your company different. Why should I want to do business with you? Break the rules all you want, as long as there is a good reason, but the values must be inviolate!

These stated values should not represent wishful thinking. They should be real and express how you act, how you work, how I can expect you to treat me consistently. The "Five Principles of Mars" (Quality, Responsibility, Mutuality, Efficiency, and Freedom) or "The Johnson and Johnson Credo" express clearly what the respective companies believe. The importance for a leadership team developing and publishing its values cannot be overstated. The rest of the organization should be asked to hold you accountable for acting consistently on your expressed values and be given the means for doing so. Only then will employees, themselves, willingly embrace the company's values.

Part of the process of having the team develop its values is to agree on ways team members can hold one another accountable for acting on the values. The only real value is one that is acted on. As a follow-on step, I often encourage teams to think about key operating principles, or Norms, by which they can operationalize the values (Appendix II lists a set of norms identified by one High Performing client). Think of these as key behaviors that would indicate whether or not the group is acting consistently on its stated values. How do your children know that you believe what you tell them is right? What do they see? If your employees observed one of your team meetings, what behaviors would they identify that would make them say you are or are not acting on your values?

Once you have identified your purpose and have agreed on what makes you tick, you are ready to decide what success looks like.

Making the Future Visible

Teams have a clearly stated vision. The vision is a graphic, agreed upon statement of what succeeding looks like. It is not three or four paragraphs of jargon-laden platitudes in which you try to summarize the quality process, your safety standards, your latest staff meeting with the board of directors, and your multiple ISO certifications. In fact, if it is too long to be hand written on the back of your business card, it is too baggy.

I avoid giving organizations examples of "good" vision statements just as I will not give them a list of "appropriate" values to assert. As soon as I hold up a vision for praise, everybody tries to ape it; just change the company's name, and plug and chug. That hardly works. There are some bad ones that are easy to spot. Ameritas Life Insurance Corporation has a two-page vision statement. It is pure pabulum and lies on the paper like a dead mouse (sorry PETA). ISP has a combination vision / mission that is a self-serving paean to the chairman. Ameritech has a clear vision that sounds very good. Living in Indiana, however, and being serviced by Ameritech and its takeover parent SBC, we know they don't mean a word of it. Because they never translated their vision to operational behaviors that impacted the customer, Ameritech attracted one negative headline after the next in Indiana newspapers throughout the year 2000 and into 2001. Ciba-Geigy Corporation has a statement that expresses wishful thinking that it will "be profitable past the year 2000." That's certainly exciting! Mobil Corporation says they want to be a "GREAT global corporation" and follows it with two sentences that say nothing about business. And Great Lakes Chemical Corporation doesn't have a vision (as is clear from their depressed stock price and profits), because the chairman thinks visions are silly.

Airborne Express gets high marks. They start with a statement of their purpose. They express their core values. Then they build the vision and express it as a direct outcome of their values:

> Quality service for our customers.
> A rewarding work environment for our people.
> Fair return to our shareholders.

And they get the order right! If they succeed in doing the first two, the third will follow naturally.

A good vision should be short and memorable. It should state the "who, what, where, when, and / or why" but not the "how." The "how" is the turf of the mission or the goals required to achieve the vision. The vision should be impervious to changes in the business cycle and describe a desired future state. It must have an enduring quality.

Strategy and Tactics for Achieving Goals

A team should have a plan to achieve the vision—it must be both strategic and tactical in nature. These considerations force the team to think about the time line involved. Is the vision for five years, three years, or next year? How soon do you want it to be obsolete? At one level, the strategy is comprised of your long-term goals to achieve your vision, say five years out; the goals are your short-term needs that must be met this year to stay on track.

The strategy is the general plan for getting from A-X. It is not the twenty-six page strategic plan that Boston Consulting put together for you. I mean a generalized statement that boils all that down into manageable bits that employees can understand and toward which they strive. The tactics are the specific intermediate goals you will try to achieve that will allow you to meet your strategic timing. Some people call this the Mission.

Establishing Metrics

High Performance Teams Establish Metrics to Ensure They Stay on Track. What gets measured gets done. There should be metrics for manufacturing and metrics for R&D, metrics for sales and metrics for marketing. Each area of the business should have specific goals to be met and metrics established to monitor the organization's path to High Performance. Managers, and employees alike, need to have a scorecard by which they can measure their progress and hold themselves accountable.

In order to achieve the vision, the team must develop a series of short and long-term goals to achieve the vision. If you have used your yearly leadership conference to develop these goals, they should be assigned to champions, measured, and their status reported back to the larger group on a monthly or quarterly basis—at the very latest, by the next annual conference.

Think of your organization with a defined purpose, clear values that people believe in, a focused vision that employees are striving to achieve, and well-publicized short and long-term goals to make it happen. Every employee knows where the organization stands because all the metrics are publicized and displayed for the organization to see.

Think of it.

CHAPTER TEN

Telling The Story

Good leaders are good storytellers. Think of your favorite novel, play, or short story. Why did you like it? Were the characters lifelike, exciting, scary, compelling, or heroic? Were they cardboard and artificial or fully fleshed out into real people that you knew or wanted to know? Were they tormented and driven like Ahab or Hamlet, seductive like Cleopatra or Lolita, sinister like Iago or Machiavelli, heroic like Anthony or Beowulf, or simply human and flawed like Holden Caulfield, Rabbit, or you and me? How about the setting? Did you like it because it was set in Jurassic Park, the house of the seven gables, Walden Pond, one of Grisham's courtrooms, a Vietnam rice paddy, or an Iraqi nerve gas factory? Did the tone or atmosphere excite you? Did you like it because the values it espoused were compatible with your own? Or was the plot the compelling feature. Were you compelled to turn one page after another from restaurants in Georgetown to Russian submarine bases because you couldn't wait to hear how it turned out, or did you plod through the last 200 pages just because you just can't stand to stop something you started? Did you immediately forget the last book you read on the red-eye from LAX to Newark, or does the rising action in the plot and the denouement (the crisis or turning point) still haunt you?

Answer these questions and you can begin to craft your organization's story. What about your company's story should attract and hold your customers' attention? What about your story compels employee loyalty?

The story of High Performance needs to be told again and again with passion and commitment. With the proper leadership and facilitation, a senior leadership team can develop its Purpose, Values, Vision, Strategy, Tactics, and Metrics in four to five days of concentrated work. Thereafter, the process needs to be rolled out to the business units, the divisions, and the manufacturing sites. Even in times of significant economic downturn, you can revolutionize your corporation inside of a year. The cost to accomplish the change will be pennies compared to the return on your investment for the time spent.

If you will gather your company's leaders once a year for a High Performance Conference for three days, you can prepare them to tell the story. Don't rely on the VP of Communications or the company magazine to tell the story.

Story telling is a leadership responsibility.

Think of a company—your company—where every employee knows the same story, tells the same story, and believes the same story. It has the same characters, plot, setting, and atmosphere. We all reach crescendo at the same time. The question is, is your story a comedy or a tragedy? High Performing Corporations have happy endings.

Let's change the metaphor. Think of your company as a holograph. The unique nature of a holograph is that if you slice it up, break it up, scatter it to sixty different locations, every one of the pieces will have 100% of the original holograph. Take your company and spread it out to sixty different countries. When every one of those sixty locations has 100% of your Purpose, Values, Vision, Strategy, Tactics, and Metrics, and tells the same exciting story, you have created High Performance.

Every organization in the world is perfectly designed to get the results it gets. If you are contented with your results, change nothing. If you are not, we invite you to join our High Performance Learning Community by visiting us at www.execustrat.com or www.williamcjeffries.com. We'll see you there!

CODA

In the light of the events that occurred in the United States on September 11, 2001, talking about business High Performance almost sounds trite. This book was initially due to be published that day. It is clear, in our consulting work since that day, the atmosphere has changed. People are more concerned about their relationships than they are about their paychecks. Seminar participants, for the longest time, were more reluctant to smile and laugh. There was a preoccupation with larger events. Even though training has once again begun, and people are going back to work physically, if not mentally, the atmosphere is still different. Everything is set into contrast against a darker background and more profound meaning.

The morning of the terrorist attack on the Twin Towers and the Pentagon, I was off to work like millions of other Americans. I drove Austin to high school at Brebeuf Jesuit and walked Paul into the International School of Indiana and said "Bonjour. Comment allez-vous?" to his teacher, Marion. My wife, Cheryl, was studying for a math test in graduate school, and Coco the dog was out back chasing a blue heron out of the waterfall. It was just one more beautiful fall morning in Zionsville, Indiana. Thousands of people went to work in the World Trade Center carrying brief cases and pictures drawn for them by their children at breakfast. Ordinary people took the train to the Pentagon to do their job. Ordinary people boarded airplanes off to family reunions, sales conferences, business meetings, and negotiations: ordinary people doing ordinary things. That very normalcy is what terrorists, in their twisted passion, strive to disrupt.

When the ordinary turned abnormal, ordinary people accomplished the extraordinary. Ordinary fire fighters, police, office mates, and passing construction workers rushed into melting buildings to rescue fellow human beings. One U. S. Navy SEAL stood outside the Pentagon and caught people jumping from burning windows in his arms until his own legs collapsed. Aboard hi-jacked United Airlines flight 93, ordinary people decided to do the extraordinary in the face of terror and uncertainty. We call them heroic.

Somehow, leaders have to craft cultures of High Performance without the horror of events like those that occurred on 911. High Performance Organizations are just groups of ordinary people who accomplish the extraordinary. The leader's task is to create a culture where such extraordinary performance is possible.

APPENDIX I

Clients
ABB Power Generation, Ltd.
Advantest America, Inc.
Aeronautical Research Laboratory (Taiwan—Republic
    of China)
AFLAC
Agfa Corporation
Ajinomoto Co, Inc., Tokyo (Japan)
Allegheny Energy
Allstates Trust Bank, Plc (Nigeria)
Alltel
All Union Foreign Economic Association
    (Technopromexport—Russia)
Alstom
Amalgamated Clothing & Textile Workers
American President Lines
America Online
American Red Cross
Ameritech
Amsterdam Airport Schiphol (The Netherlands)
Ansys, Inc.
Array Technology Corporation
Arthur Anderson
Asheboro, N. C. Public Schools
Asian Peroxides, Ltd.
AT&T
Austrian Energy (Austria)
Bahrain Institute of Banking and Finance (Bahrain)
Ball State University
The Bank of Butterfield (Bermuda)
Bank Ekspor Impor Indonesia Bankexim (Indonesia)
Bank Indonesia (Indonesia)
Banco Itau S. A. (Brazil)
Banco Real de Investimento S/A (Brazil)
Barama Company, Ltd. (Guyana)
Bay Area Rapid Transit
Bay Networks
Bayer Corporation

Be Free Inc.
Bell Laboratories
Bell Northern Research (Canada)
Bell South
Bethlehem Steel Corporation
BitWise Solutions
Blue Cross Blue Shield
Boeing Company
BP Exploration (UK)
BP Oil International, Ltd. (Malaysia)
Bristol-Myers Squibb
British Airways, Gatwick, (UK)
Brooke Bond Lipton India, Ltd. (India)
Brown and Williamson
Byers Engineering
Cadillac Products
Capital Market Board (Turkey)
Carborundum Universal, Ltd. (India)
Caterpillar Corporation
Cavill Power Products Pty., Ltd., (Australia)
Celanese
Centeon
Central Intelligence Agency
Chase Manhattan Bank
Chem Design Corporation
Chemical Bank
Chevrolet Motor Division
Chevron Petroleum Technology Company
Chevron Real Estate management Company
Christopher Newport College
Cia. Vale Do Rio Doce, Rio De Janeiro (Brazil)
CIBA Vision
Cigna Corporation
Clarion
Colorado Springs Utilities
Cominco American Inc.
Computer Science Corporation
Conoco, Inc.
Coromandel Engineering Co., Ltd. (India)
COSA
Croon Elektrotechniek B. V. (Netherlands)

CTR Systems
Crompton Corporation
Cummins Komatsu Engine Co
Davis-Standard Corporation
Defense Information Systems Agency
Defense Mapping Agency
Defense Nuclear Agency
Deloitte & Touche
Delphi Automotive Systems
Delta
Dentsu, Inc. (Japan)
Digital Equipment Corporation, U.S. & (Germany)
DLG (East Jutland)
D. M. Swagerman Advies B. V. (Netherlands)
Duquesne Power & Light Co
Duracell
Dupont de Nemours
East Africa Industries Limited (Kenya)
Eastern Associated Coal Corporation
Eastman Kodak
Eicher, Ltd. (India)
E. I. D. Parry, Ltd. (India)
Ensalso (Italy)
EPDC, Electric Power Development Co. Ltd.
Ernst & Young
Eveready
Federal Executive Institute
Federal Ministry for the Environment, Nature & Nuclear
    Safety (Germany)
FEMA
First Funding Corporation
Fisher Scientific International, Inc
Ford Motor Company
Foreign Broadcast Information Service
Freeport McMoran Copper & Gold
Freightliner Corporation
GAF
General Motors Corporation
GM Powertrain, Strasbourg (France)
GM Truck Group
General Railway Signal Corporation

Genstar, Inc.
Georgia Power
Geoserve—CITG
Giben America
Godrej Soaps Limited (India)
Goodyear Tire & Rubber Co.
Gough, Gough, & Hamer, Ltd. (New Zealand)
Government Property Agency, Hong Kong Government
    (Hong Kong)
Great Lakes Chemical Corporation
Hampton Roads Publishing Company
Harris Chemical Group
Haworth International
Hewlett-Packard (Latin American Division)
Heinz
Himachal Futuristic Communications, Ltd. (India)
Hindustan Lever, Ltd. (India)
Hoechst, A.G. (Germany)
Honeywell, Inc.
Hong Kong Government (China)
Hoogovens Steel (The Netherlands)
IBM
IBM (Uruguay)
Ida (Ireland)
IMC
Imperial Chemicals Industries, Plc.(UK)
Institute of Nuclear Power Operators
International Management Institute (Ukraine)
International Services Limited (Nigeria)
International Specialty Products, U. S. (Singapore, Brazil,
    Belgium)
ISI-Dentsu (Japan)
Israel Credit Cards (Israel)
ITESM (Mexico)
Itochu Corporation, Jakarta (Indonesia), Japan
J. R. Simplot Company
Jemico Group of Companies (Uganda)
Joy Mining Machinery
Kolon Industries—Fiber Production (Korea)
Komatsu Ltd. (Japan)
Legent Corporation

Lisberg—CJ Management (Denmark)
L. K. Comstock & Company, Inc.
Lockheed Martin (all divisions)
Lucent Technologies
Macmahon Holdings Ltd. (South Australia)
Maha Rasta Apex Corporation, Ltd.
Mallinckrodt, Inc.
Marconi
Mastech Corporation
Matsa Lumber Company
Mattell Interactive
Mead
Medrad, Inc.
Merck and Co.
Merrill Lynch
Messier Dowty Aerospace
Milliken & Company
Millipore
Minaj Nigeria Limited (Nigeria)
Mingledorf
Ministry of Welfare, Government of India (India)
Mitsubishi Heavy Industries, Ltd. (Japan)
Mitsubishi Motors
Mobil Oil Co, Ltd. (UK)
Murex Investments
Murugappa Group (India)
National Imagery and Mapping Agency (NIMA)
National Mediation Board
National Reconnaissance Office
National Security Agency
National Westminster Bank, PLC (England)
Naval Sea Systems Command
NCR
New York Transit Authority
Nihon Unisys, Ltd. (Japan)
Norfolk Collegiate School, Norfolk, Virginia
North American Chemical Corporation
Office of the Chaplain, USMA
OHM Remediation
Old Dominion University
Orbisphere Labs

Oriental Brewery Co., Ltd. (Korea)
PACCAR Technical Center
Pacific Bell
Pantone, Inc.
Parry Agro Industries, Ltd.
Performance Contracting Corporation
Performance Solutions
Per-Se Technologies
Petroleum Corporation of Jamaica, (Jamaica, W. I.)
Pfizer Corporation
Photocircuits Corporation
Physitron Corporation
PNC Bank
PPG Industries
Price Waterhouse
PT Sriboga Raturaya (Indonesia)
Quest International (Japan)
Rail Transportation Systems, Inc.
Ramon & Demm
Raychem, Ltd.
Rayonier, Inc.
Regents University
Regions Bank
Rhone Poulenc (France)
Rock Hill, South Carolina Public Schools
Roland Berger and Partners, GmbH. (Germany)
Rolls Royce. Plc (UK)
Roman Catholic Diocese of Virginia
Rompetrol (Rumania)
The Rouse Corporation
Roussell Uclef (France)
RPS, Inc.
Samsung Electronics Co, Ltd.
SASIB Railway GRS
SASOL (PTY) Ltd. (South Africa)
Sastech Pty., Ltd.
Saudi Arabian Oil Co. (Saudi Arabia)
SBC
Scientex, L. C.
Scientific Atlanta
Semeg, Ltd. (Brazil)

Senior Executive Institute
Sharp Laboratories of Europe (England)
Shin Caterpillar Mitsubishi
Shindler Management, Ltd.
Singapore Government
Sona Steering Systems, Ltd.
Southern Company
South Iron, Missouri, School System
South Trust Bank
Southwestern Bell Communications
Space and Naval Warfare Systems
SPIRC
Spirit Cruise Lines
Sprint
State Bank of Mauritius (Mauritius)
Sterling Software
Sumitomo Chemical Co., Ltd. (Japan)
Sumitomo Osaka Cement Co., Ltd. (Japan)
Sun Microsystems, Inc. (Hong Kong)
Sun Trust
Tata Exports, Ltd. (India)
Tata Iron and Steel Company (India)
Teamsters, International
Teijin Ltd. (Japan)
Telecordia Technologies
Texaco (Latin America / West Africa)
Texas Instruments
The Timkin Company
Thermacore International, Inc.
Thiokol Corporation
Ticona
TJ Diamond Chain, Ltd. (India)
Transarc Corporation
Tube Instruments of India, Ltd. (India)
Uarco, Inc.
Unilever-Algida-Iglo (Poland)
Unilever (Netherlands)
Union Switch and Signal
Uniroyal Chemical
United Bank of India
United Methodist Services For the Aging

U. S. Air Force
U. S. Airways
U. S. APCA
U. S. Army
U. S. Department of Agriculture
U. S. Department of Commerce
U. S. Department of Defense
U. S. Department of Health and Human Services
U. S. Department of the Interior, Water Resources Board
U. S. Department of State
U. S. Environmental Protection Agency
U. S. Marine Corps
U. S. Navy Seals
U. S. Navy Explosive Ordinance Disposal
U. S. Postal Service
U. S. Silica
U. S. Steel
U. S. X
United Way
Virginia Association of Independent Schools
Vista Chemical Co.
Wacker Siltronics Corporation
Watkins-Johnson Co.
Wells Fargo Bank
Weltravel (Germany)
Western States Machine Co.
West Virginia Expert Teachers Academy
Xerox Corporation
Zionsville, Indiana, Public School System.

I am also indebted to tens of thousands of graduate and undergraduate students and numerous business professionals at several universities where I have taught who have questioned, debated, argued, challenged, and, in other exciting ways, helped to refine my ideas over the years:

The Armed Forces Staff College
Ball State University
Brussels International School
Carnegie Mellon University, Graduate School of Industrial Administration

Christopher Newport College
Georgetown University Medical Center
Georgia Tech University, Dupree School of Management
Industrial College of the Armed Forces
INSEAD
Louisiana State University
National Defense University, Personal Development
    Programs
Old Dominion University, Graduate School of Education
Regents University
University of Georgia, Regions Leadership University
The University of Richmond
University of Southern California, Graduate Business
    School
University of Pittsburgh, Management in Technology
    Organizations
United States Army Command and General Staff College
United States Military Academy, West Point
United States Naval War College.

APPENDIX II

Team Norms

I don't hold these out as a model for the best norms a team can have but as an example of norms that were developed by one group of High Performing individuals, all of whom went at least as high as General Manager level.

- We will encourage and accept risks
- All ideas will be welcome
- We will practice confidentiality
- We will model our team values in our personal lives
- Everyone will participate and contribute
- We will come to meeting prepared
- We will not prejudge
- We will challenge and support team mates
- We will ensure an opportunity to prepare
- We will stay focused. When we are here, we will be present
- We will hold one meeting at a time. We will hold no side bar meetings
- We will begin on time and end on time
- We will have fun and enjoy our experience together
- It's OK to say "I'm uncomfortable with this discussion."
- It's OK to suggest changing our agenda and our approach
- We will extend our norms to our guests

What a Leader Does

1. Break the Huddle
2. Check the play clock
3. Identify the defensive personnel
4. Check the number of defensive backs (3, 4, or 5)
5. Determine the defensive alignment
6. Identify Mike (middle linebacker); he keys the pass coverage
7. Call out Mike
8. Ensure the center identifies Mike and makes the correct line call
9. Check the safeties (1 safety = man-to-man coverage; 2 safeties = probably zone coverage)
10. Check your ten teammates for their alignment
11. Check the play clock again
12. Watch the defense
13. Note the shifts going on
14. Feel the blitz
15. Check off if necessary
16. Recheck alignment
17. Check the play clock again
18. Start the snap count
19. Check the motion man
20. DETONATION!

And you thought you had it tough. What I find interesting about this checklist is that only five items actually involve your own organization. Fifteen involve the competition or the marketplace.

BIBLIOGRAPHY

Abrams, Jeffrey. *The Mission Statement Book*. New York: Ten Speed Press, 1995.

Beckhard, Richard, and Wendy Pritchard. *Changing the Essence: The Art of Creating and Leading Fundamental Change in Organizations*. San Francisco: Jossey-Bass Publishers, 1992.

Birch, Alex, Philipp Gerber, and Dirk Schneider. *The Age of E-Tail*. Oxford: Capstone Publishing, 2000.

Bridges, William. *The Character of Organizations*. Palo Alto: Davies-Black Publishing, Co., 2000.

Eliot, Dr. Robert S. and Dennis L. Breo. *Is It Worth Dying For?* New York: Bantam, 1984.

Fisher, Roger, and William Ury. *Getting to Yes: Negotiating Without Giving In*. New York: Penguin Books, 1981.

Hanna, David P. *Designing Organizations for High Performance*. *Reading*: Addison-Wesley Publishing Company, 1988.

Ikujiro, Nonaka and Hirotaka Takeuchi. *The Knowledge Creating Company*. New York: Oxford Press, 1995.

Jeffries, William C. *Taming the Scorpion: Preparing American Business For the Third Millennium*. Chapel Hill, NC: Professional Press, 1996.

_____. *True To Type: Answers to the Most Frequently Asked Questions About Interpreting the Myers-Briggs Type Indicator*.® Charlottesville, VA: Hampton Roads Publishing, 1990.

Jennings, Jason and Laurence Haughton. *It's not the BIG that eat SMALL... it's the FAST that eat the SLOW.* New York: Harper Business, 2000.

Kelley, Robert E. *How to be a Star at Work.* New York: Random House, 1998.

Kotter, John P. *A Force For Change: How Leadership Differs From Management.* New York: The Free Press, 1990.

_____. *Leading Change.* Boston: Harvard Business School Press, 1996.

Kuhn, Thomas S. *The Structure of Scientific Revolutions.* 2d ed. Chicago: The University of Chicago, 1962.

Machiavelli, Niccolo. *The Prince.* Trans. By George Bull. New York: Penguin, 1999.

McCall, Morgan W., Michael M. Lombardo, and Ann M. Morrison. *The Lessons of Experience: How Successful Executives Develop on the Job.* Lexington, MA: Lexington Books, 1988.

Modal, Mary. *Now or Never.* New York: Harper Business, 2000.

Neff, Thomas J. and James M. Citrin. *Lessons From the Top.* New York: Doubleday, 1999.

Peters, Tom. *Liberation Management.* New York: Alfred A. Knopf, 1992.

Phillips, Donald T. *Lincoln on Leadership.* New York: Warner Books, 1992.

Ross, Gerald. *Toppling the Pyramids.* New York: Random House, 1994.

Rummler, Geary A. and Alan P. Brache. *Improving Performance: How to Manage the White Space on the Organization Chart.* San Francisco: Jossey-Bass, 1990.

Schein, Edgar H. *Career Anchors.* San Diego: Pfeiffer & Company, 1990.

Siegel, David. *Futurize Your Enterprise: Business Strategy in the Age of the E-Customer.* New York: John Wiley & Sons, Inc., 1999.

Senge, Peter. *The Fifth Discipline: The Art and Practice of the Learning Organization.* New York: Doubleday, 1990.

_____. *The Fifth Discipline Fieldbook.* New York: Doubleday, 1994.

Useem, Michael. *The Leadership Moment.* New York: Three Rivers Press, 1998.

Weisbord, Marvin R. Productive Workplaces: *Organizing and Managing for Dignity, Meaning, and Community.* San Francisco: Jossey-Bass Publishers, 1990.

About The Author

William C. Jeffries is an international consultant and master teacher who specializes in human and organizational behavior. He has been a soldier, scholar, university professor, editor, business leader, and trusted personal coach for prominent leaders around the world. Currently, as the President and Chief Executive Officer of Executive Strategies International, Inc., he leads a diverse team of consultants with interdisciplinary backgrounds who bring global perspectives to the workplace of the future. His undergraduate studies at the United States Military Academy at West Point were in engineering and management, his post graduate work in Germany was in nuclear engineering, and his graduate work at Duke University was in language, literature, and values.

His clientele include an international who's who of public officials, Fortune 500 companies, professional athletes, government agencies, universities, the armed forces, public and private schools, and the media in 19 countries. He has developed and taught programs on Leadership In A Changing World for such organizations as Carnegie Mellon University, Hoechst AG, The Boeing Company, The Federal Executive Institute, Bayer, Eastman Kodak, Caterpillar, Digital, Banco Itau, S.A., Unilever, Capital Market Board, General Motors, Hoogovens Steel, PPG, Merck, ISP Singapore & Brazil, BP, Komatsu International, Pfizer, The Senior Executive Association, Lockheed Martin, Ga. Tech, Regions Bank, Rolls Royce, Plc., Lucent Technologies, United Methodist Services for the Aging, and The Department of Defense.

Bill provides counsel as an Executive Coach and consults with the senior leadership of numerous corporations and organizations including, Virgin Airlines, BART, The Environmental Protection Agency, Nuclear Regulatory Commission, Lockheed Martin, North American Chemical Corporation, CIA, Pfizer Pharmaceuticals, U. S. Army, Hewlett Packard, Crompton Corporation, AGFA

Corporation, Performance Contracting Group, The Food and Drug Administration, Bayer Corporation, Israel Card, AT&T, PNC Bank, Regions Financial Corporation, IBM, Hoechst, AG, National Bank of Kuwait, New York Transit Authority, SBC, Digital Corporation, Rhone Poulenc, Celanese Corporation, Millipore, Medrad, Raychem, J. R. Simplot, Bristol-Myers Squibb, Spirit Cruise Lines, and the U. S. Navy.

In addition to his consulting activities, Bill also advises and teaches in several school systems including The Virginia Association of Independent Schools, South Iron, Missouri Public Schools, West Virginia Expert Teachers Academy, Rockhill, South Carolina Public Schools, and the Zionsville, Indiana Public Schools. Bill also teaches in the Graduate School of Education of Old Dominion University, and the Business Schools at USC, The University of Pittsburgh, and The University of Georgia. He is also an adjunct faculty member of the Naval War College in the Department of Strategic Studies, The DuPree School of Management at Georgia Tech, and the Graduate School of Industrial Administration at Carnegie Mellon University, where for 10 years he has been the most highly rated professor in The Program for Executives, the program rated by *The Wall Street Journal* as the World's Finest Program for Developing Effective Global Executive Leadership.

Bill has written on subjects as diverse as New Business Development, Business High Performance, Organizational Change, Russian Literature, Human Ethnology, War and Morality, Poetry, Professional Ethics, Modern American Fiction, Psychological Type, and the Development of High Performance Teams. His book entitled *True To Type* is widely used in several countries as an organizational leader's guide to personality diversity, and his book, *Taming the Scorpion: Preparing Business for the Third Millennium* is used as a leader's guide to developing high performance organizations. He is currently writing two more books: one on corporate techniques for "Developing a Strategic Business Sense," and a war novel set in Laos and Cambodia.

In his consulting work, Bill specializes in Organizational Change. He regularly works with corporations to assist them in instituting major organizational changes, developing cultures that support self-managed work teams, and fostering partnering relationships between customers and suppliers. He frequently is called in to assist in wholesale reengineering efforts of manufacturing sites, corporate-wide diversity initiatives, and the change leadership efforts required to make the implementation of SAP and other enterprise-wide changes more effective.

Bill is affiliated with several scholarly and professional organizations including The American Chamber of Commerce in Belgium, The Association of Psychological Type, America's Promise, Association for the Management of Organizational Design, The Honor Society of Phi Kappa Phi, The Joint Services Conference on Professional Ethics, The Indianapolis Chamber of Commerce, ASTD, and the Martin Luther King House.